Glacier National Park for Families

Alex Neill

© 2016 Alex Neill
A & M Expeditions, LLC

ISBN: 978-0-9889549-6-0

Library of Congress Control Number: 2016933878

First edition, April 2016

Published in the United States Of America
Printed in South Korea
by Four Colours Print Group, Loiusville, Kentucky

All Rights Reserved

No part of this book may be reproduced or transmitted in any form or by any means, electronic or mechanical, including photocopying, recording or by any information storage or retrieval system, without written permission from the copyright owner or the publisher except for brief quotations in a review.

Unattributed quotations and photographs are from Alex Neill

Distributed by:
Montana Outdoor Guidebooks, LLC
175 Hutton Ranch Rd., Ste. 103
Kalispell, MT 59901
www.climbglacier.com
info@climbglacier.com

Dedication

I dedicate this book to my husband and two daughters. Our children have been our motivation to explore and enjoy Glacier National Park to show them all that it offers. None of this would have been possible without the help of my husband. May our children remember their childhood in the mountains, and use their experience as motivation to explore for the rest of their lives.

Table of Contents:

Chapter 1: Introduction	2
Chapter 2: Ranger-Led Activity Schedule, Shuttles, Tours, and Activities	6
Chapter 3: Going-to-the-Sun Road and Logan Pass	16
Chapter 4: West Glacier, Apgar, and Lake McDonald	24
Chapter 5: East Glacier and Two Medicine	38
Chapter 6: Many Glacier	50
Chapter 7: St. Mary	68
Chapter 8: The North Fork, Bowman Lake, and Kintla Lake	79
Chapter 9: Activities Outside of Glacier National Park	86
Chapter 10: Winter in Glacier National Park	98
Chapter 11: Know Before You Go	102
Chapter 12: Equipment and What to Bring	110
Chapter 13: Equipment for Young Children	118
Chapter 14: Sample Itineraries	122

The author enjoying Running Eagle Falls

Foreword by Blake Passmore

Some of my fondest memories have been made in Glacier National Park.

As a child I would accompany my parents and extended family on trips to Avalanche Lake and Logan Pass. I especially remember picnic lunches with my grandparents who must have loved the park; they honeymooned in the Two Medicine Valley in 1923.

As an avid writer, photographer, and climber, I have been blessed to continue this love affair with Glacier, but everyone I go with carries their own gear. Alex brings insight as a mom who takes her family to some of Glacier's most amazing places with kids on their backs!

Glacier for Families will help your family start to develop your own great memories in Glacier National Park. This book will be especially helpful if your family just has a few days to spend in this spectacular place. There is a lot to do, and Alex makes recommendations about what to see and how to see it as well as give detailed gear recomendations.

Alex has personally hiked to each place she recommends and has lots of helpful tips and insider suggestions to help you get the most out of your trip to Glacier National Park, The Crown of the Continent.

Be safe out there.

Blake Passmore
Kalispell, MT
Author and photographer
www.climbglacier.com

View from the trail to St. Mary Falls

Chapter One: Introduction

Most people who have heard of Glacier National Park have a vision of standing on the shores of Lake McDonald at Apgar and driving over Logan Pass via Going-to-the-Sun Road. While those things should be on your to-do list, I hope this book encourages you to branch out and see more of Glacier than Lake McDonald, St. Mary Lake, and Going-to-the-Sun Road. There is so much to see and do in this national park that is enjoyable for families and those with children.

This book is written for those of us who want more than just a road trip over Going-to-the-Sun Road, but who, due to age, time constraints, or little ones in tow, may not be able to tackle daunting hikes like Pitamakan Pass or Sperry Chalet. For those of us in search of breathtaking picnic spots secluded from the masses at Apgar Village, but do not have the means or ability to climb some of the larger mountains in the park.

Glacier National Park offers so much more than the famous Going-to-the-Sun Road, and you do not have to be a mountain climber or backcountry expert to explore and enjoy it. Every hike discussed and nearly every photo shared in this book was taken with a toddler and/or a newborn cooing nearby.

My family is fortunate to live minutes from Glacier, so we are lucky enough to explore a little bit at a time, not forced to pick a few things to do on a short vacation. This book guides families toward the best things to do during your visit. While you may have to pick and choose depending on the length of your stay, this book provides you with the information to make your stay the best for you and your family.

Flowers in the meadows of Logan Pass
Photo courtesy of Blake Passmore

I grew up in Kalispell, Montana, not far from the West Entrance to Glacier. I will often refer to Glacier National Park as "Glacier" or "the Park" in this book, not only for abbreviation purposes, but also because that is what we call it on a daily basis as we peer in awe toward the looming peaks to the east.

My love for Glacier began early in life, when we would take grade school field trips to Avalanche Lake, and spend summers learning at the Glacier Institute and driving to Logan Pass. I began college as a Biology major, thinking that I may want to be a park ranger upon my return to Montana. I ended up becoming an attorney, and more recently a full-time mom, so my exploration of Glacier is never as full-time as I want it to be. And yet having little ones has allowed me to really enjoy the subtle treasures in the Park.

Alex, Matt, and their family

My husband and I now reside in Whitefish, Montana. We have been blessed with two beautiful little girls, one born in 2012 and one born in 2014. We have taken them hiking and exploring all over Glacier, and thus can provide the firsthand information you need to have a safe and wonderful visit to Glacier with your family. You can follow more of our adventures on our website, "Montana Vacation Blog," that provides more information, stories, and photos about the entire beautiful state of Montana: montanavacationblog.com.

This book provides a lot of information a person traveling with a family might need when visiting Glacier. From what to bring, where to stay, whether there is cell service, where to hike, and family fun just outside the Park, this book includes what every family needs when visiting the Park.

I also discuss several products, gear, and park vendors throughout the book. I have not received any compensation for mentioning them here. Their inclusion is simply because it is what we have used or experienced personally, and if I endorse a particular product or vendor, it simply means it worked for my family and me!

There are plenty of books out there for the person who is looking to climb the beautiful and challenging peaks in Glacier, and for those thrill-seekers, this is not the right book. This book covers beautiful hikes and things to do for those that might not want to spend a week in the backcountry or climb the huge peaks available in the park.

There are also a lot of books and websites describing with GPS exactitude every inch of all 700-plus miles of hiking trails in the Park. You will not find that type of information here either - although the "hiking" sections provide all the information you need to navigate the 20-plus family friendly hikes described in this book. What you will find here is first hand knowledge crucial for families visiting Glacier, with personal recommendations for experiences you can and should pursue on your visit.

Finally, this "guidebook" is written in first-person, as my hope is that seeing a multitude of memorable experiences another family has experienced will inspire you to take in more than just Going-to-the-Sun Road. For instance, one of my blog followers asked me about taking her 6-month old on the ten-mile round trip hike to beautiful Iceberg Lake. The answer? You bet!

I have tried to personalize the book so that you know about some "don't miss" family hikes, but also some I would not recommend. For instance, the picture on the cover is of my husband and our two-year old on the Highline Trail. This hike is one of the best hiking trails in Glacier National Park, but I don't consider this to be a family-friendly hike, as it is actually quite dangerous for little ones or anyone not stable on their feet. Our experience is described in a later chapter. An impersonal guidebook might not be so frank.

Lake McDonald

Best Times to Visit

This book focuses on things that are mostly open during the summer months of May/June to September.

To learn more about winter in Glacier National Park, see Chapter Ten: Winter in Glacier National Park.

While you can still visit Glacier National Park during the winter months, due to the snow; you will be unable to drive over Logan Pass which connects West Glacier to East Glacier via Going-to-the-Sun Road. Logan Pass is usually not accessible until the end of June or beginning of July, depending on snow. Because fewer visitors visit the park in the winter, most of the businesses shut down during those months, so don't count on being able to do everything in this book during the winter months.

Spring at Logan Pass

Safety in the Park

It is easy to forget while visiting Glacier that this beautiful, popular destination can also be dangerous. While you may be surrounded by other visitors, remember that you are in the wild and you should act accordingly.

Here are a few things to keep in mind:

The animals are not pets.

The animals in Glacier National Park are wild. They may be accustomed to having a lot of humans around, but that does not mean it is safe to approach them. You should also never feed any wildlife in the park. I always carry bear spray as a safety precaution, no matter where I am at in Glacier Park, and you should do the same.

The water is cold, fast and dangerous.

The lakes and rivers in Glacier are fed from the melting snow on the mountains and glaciers. Expect the water to be ice cold, even in the middle of the summer when the weather is hot. The river water runs fast, particularly during the spring and early summer with the runoff from the melting snow. Do not get too close to fast-moving water, and do not stay in cold water for long. Death by drowning is one of the leading causes of death in the park.

Do not hike alone.

It is important for someone to know at all times where you are. Most visitors traveling with families do not find themselves completely alone. But be sure to let someone know your plan for the day, or travel with other adults who are able to get help if you are hiking and need someone to get back alone.

I want to personally welcome you to Glacier National Park. I hope you enjoy your stay and may you return more than once.

Hiking in the fall on the Swiftcurrent Pass Trail

Chapter Two: Ranger-Led Activity Schedule, Shuttles, Tours, and Activities

This chapter covers the various activities available within Glacier National Park. There are guided hikes, boat tours, boat rentals, and horseback riding available within the Park. There are also Sun Tours and Red Bus Tours offered for a fee, and Glacier National Park also offers a free shuttle service along Going-to-the-Sun Road.

In July and August, Glacier offers a variety of "ranger-led activities" for the entire family to enjoy. These include guided hikes, special presentations, evening programs, drop-in programs, and guided boat tours. These are a great way for your family to learn more about Glacier National Park with a ranger, and most of the programs are free, with the exception of the boat tours and some of the Native America Speaks programs. The Glacier Institute is a local non-profit organization that offers many types of classes and programs for people of all ages.

Details on the activities available in each area of the park are discussed in each respective chapter.

Presentations and Evening Programs

Glacier offers talks and evening programs throughout the park at various locations, including campgrounds. These programs cover a variety of topics, and are free. Some programs are particularly wonderful for families, and they are sure to be fun and educational. Check the Ranger-Led Activity Schedule available at park entrances and visitor centers for times and programs.

Junior Ranger Program

The Junior Ranger program is a wonderful program for children to learn more about Glacier while earning their official Glacier Junior Ranger badge. Children wishing to obtain their badge must complete a free Junior Ranger Activity Booklet, and then turn it in to a ranger to take an oath and receive their badge. The activity booklets can be picked up at the St. Mary, Logan Pass, or Apgar Visitor Centers, or the Apgar Nature Center located in the Apgar Village. Some of the activities include connecting the dots, matching, crosswords, and short answer questions about the geology, ecosystems, and species in Glacier National Park.

Junior Rangers are typically ages 5 – 13, but anyone can participate. If you have young children who are not able to read yet, they also have a pre-reader version for the youngest Junior Rangers. And adults, don't be shy about participating also!

There is a Junior Ranger Discovery Talk and a Junior Ranger Explorer Walk that take place in Apgar Village. See the chapter on Apgar and Lake McDonald for more.

Drop-In Programs

Glacier offers various drop-in programs throughout the summer season. The Park has rangers available for various programs that you can drop by between certain hours if you are interested in hearing about specific topics.

Swiftcurrent Lake

Drop-in programs are only available in the Apgar area and at Logan Pass. Read those sections of the book for available drop-in programs. An example of a drop-in program is the Apgar Nature Center.

Instameets and Photo Walks

A few new programs offered that began in 2015 are Instameets and photo walks. For anyone who uses Instagram, an instameet is a set meeting for like-minded people to get together and take photos or to talk about Glacier. Photo walks are a fun gathering for short walks to take photos with rangers and other visitors.

There are a few Instameets and photo walks offered each month. Be sure to check the Ranger-Led Activity Schedule for the month you are visiting to find out when these are available. If you attend one of these, be sure to use the hashtag, **#GlacierNPS**, on Instagram to tag your photos.

Ranger-Led Hikes

Ranger-led hikes are a great way to do some of the hikes in Glacier with a free, guided tour. These hikes provide interesting information about the ecology, geology, history and other interesting tidbits by expert rangers who have intimate knowledge about Glacier. This is also a great option for anyone who may be nervous about going alone, worried about animals, or potentially getting lost.

There are some downsides to hiking with a group as well. The ranger stops the group quite often to speak about various topics. Sometimes this may be in the hot summer sun. When hiking with children, it is nice to be flexible and stop and go as you need to. Because you have to hike at the pace set by the ranger, this aspect may be difficult for those with small children. We have seen some ranger-led hikes that had 30 or more people, so this is something else to keep in mind if hiking in relative solitude is important to you.

You will want to be prepared whenever doing any level of hike in Glacier, and participating in any of the guided hikes is no exception. Bring food, water, layered clothing for the possibility of change of weather, and appropriate footwear.

Ranger-led hikes take place on many trails throughout Glacier Park; examples include Avalanche Lake, Aster Park, Scenic Point, Iceberg Lake and Grinnell Glacier.

Boat Tours

Morning Eagle on Lake Josephine

Boat tours are offered in Glacier on St. Mary Lake, Two Medicine Lake, Swiftcurrent Lake and Lake Josephine at Many Glacier, and Lake McDonald at Lake McDonald Lodge. These tours are offered by the Glacier Park Boat Company, a historic company that has been doing tours in Glacier National Park since the 1930's.

Boat tours are a great way for families to not only enjoy another aspect of the Park, but it can also be a way to shave off several miles of hiking by taking boats on certain trails. Children will enjoy the wooden boats, and your captain will provide a talking tour of the history of the vessel and the area on each trip. The commentary is interesting, fun, and entertaining for all.

These boat tours are also a great place to take photographs. The windows on the boat open for fresh air and pictures. You are also allowed to walk out on the front deck of the boat for photos.

Some of the boat tours also offer guided hiking tours at no additional charge.

For more information on each particular boat tour, see the chapter on the area you want to take a boat tour. Call (406) 257-2426 for reservations. Each tour has to be reserved in advance to be guaranteed a spot, so book as soon as you can.

Boat Rentals

The Glacier Boat Company offers boats for rent at Apgar, Lake McDonald Lodge, Two Medicine and Many Glacier. All of their locations offer canoes, rowboats, and single and double kayaks for rent. Lake McDonald at Apgar also has motorboats for rent.

Life jackets are provided at no additional cost. There is a one-hour minimum charge on all rental boats, and rentals are available on a first-come, first-serve basis.

Boat rental season runs from the beginning of June through the middle of September. Hours vary at each location.

Boats for rent at Apgar

Apgar Nature Center

Formerly known as the "Discovery Cabin," the Apgar Nature Center is located in the Apgar village at the base of Lake McDonald. There is a parking lot across from Eddie's, and you will see a sign pointing to a pathway through the woods. There are mountain lion "tracks" you will follow to the cabin.

Apgar Nature Center

From the end of June through Labor Day, the Nature Center is staffed with park rangers who can help you explore the various cabin items, including sorting rocks, horns, and antlers, and stamping animals into their proper habitats. The animals that were on display at the old Visitor Center in Apgar (the Visitor Center recently moved locations out of the village closer to the West Entrance) are now on display at the Nature Center. This is great interaction for kids to feel a wolf's coat or to touch a grizzly bear's claws. There is also a mystery touch box, and children can create their own puppet shows.

The Apgar Nature Center is also where you check out the Family Packs – see the next section for more information on these. This is also one of the locations for "drop-in" programs.

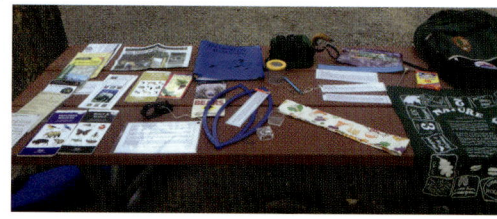

"Family Pack" contents

Family Packs

Glacier offers a free 24-hour "Family Pack" rental at the Apgar and St. Mary Visitor Centers from mid-June to mid-September. This engaging backpack is full of fun activities for your kids to explore more of Glacier National Park. Some of the contents include a compass, ruler, thermometer, bug box, binoculars, and guides on birds, animal tracks, and wildflowers, amongst many other items. This is a fun way to keep your children entertained while you are camping!

These packs are first-come, first-served. At Apgar, the Family Pack may be at the Apgar Nature Center rather than the Visitor Center. They are supposed to be returned to the Apgar Nature Center but sometimes get returned to the Visitor Center.

Do not be concerned if some rangers or park staff has no idea what you are talking about when you mention the Family Pack. It seems that only the rangers who check them in and out are familiar with them.

Glacier Institute Programs

The Glacier Institute is a private nonprofit that provides educational adventures in Glacier National Park and the Flathead National Forest bordering the Park. Their field-based programs are a fantastic way for children and adults to get into the wilderness and learn about a variety of topics from knowledgeable instructors in winter and summer. I was able to participate in several of these programs when I was a kid, and I highly recommend them as a summer camp that is educational!

Big Creek

There are programs for kids, or programs for the entire family. For more information, contact the Glacier Institute at glacierinstitute.org, or by phone at (406) 755-1211.

Native America Speaks

The Native America Speaks program is a generous group of Blackfeet, Salish, Kootenai, and Pend d'Oreille tribal members who share their intimate knowledge about the Native American history and culture at campgrounds, lodges, and the St. Mary Visitor Center. These tribes are located just outside the park boundaries, and played a significant role in shaping the history and culture of Glacier.

Two highlights of this program are Jack Gladstone's talk and the Two Medicine Lake Singers and Dancers. Jack Gladstone is a native PoetSinger of the Blackfeet Indian Nation, and he combines songs and narrative to tell the history of the area. Be sure to check the Native America Speaks schedule to find exact dates and locations for each month and year.

You can find the current schedule for the Native America Speaks programs at **nps.gov/glac/planyourvisit/nas.htm**.

I find the Native America Speaks programs to be some of the most fascinating and attention-getting talks of all of the programs in Glacier National Park.

Red Bus Tours

The Red Bus Tours are the only ground transportation in Glacier National Park that also include a tour. Many of the red buses currently operating have been in service since the 1930's. Most tours operate from the end of June through the end of September.

The famous red buses have roll back tops, allowing guests to breathe in the fresh air and get the best views while touring the scenery in and around the park. There are no seatbelts in the buses.

A Red Bus at Logan Pass

Prices vary depending on the tour you choose, but children are generally half the price of the adults. Children under age two ride free in the lap of an adult, but you must still make a reservation for them. Full payment is required at the time of reservation. Tour times vary in length from 2 up to 8 hours.

There are several options for tours. The tours depart from several hotels on the east and west side of Glacier National Park. Check the pick-up places for your specific tour when booking.

It is <u>very important to bring your park pass or park entrance receipt on the tour.</u> Many tours will exit and then re-enter the park, and the fee for your tour does not include the park entrance fee. Check in at the desk at the pickup location at least 15 minutes before departure.

If you are looking for a fun way to see and learn about the park without having to drive Going-to-the-Sun Road yourself, this is a wonderful option. The only reason you might not want to do a tour is when you are traveling with small children. I personally like to be flexible and on my own schedule with little ones.

Sun Tours

The Glacier National Park Sun Tour is a tour provided by Blackfeet Nation residents that provide Blackfeet tribal history and culture, from the spiritual history to the commonly used plants and roots for medicine. These are air-conditioned coach buses that seat up to 25 people.

The Sun Tour departs from East Glacier, Browning, St. Mary, and West Glacier. Reservations are accepted in advance, or up to the day before.

For more information and to book a tour, call (800) 786-9220.

The Sun Tour website is glaciersuntours.com/GlacierParkTours.html.

FREE Shuttle Service

A free shuttle service is offered along Going-to-the-Sun Road. The Glacier National Park shuttle system is generally open from July 1 through the first week of September, dependent on weather. The shuttle is a great option for those who are afraid to drive Going-to-the-Sun Road, that want to have their eyes on the scenery rather than glued to the road, or who don't want to deal with the limited parking available at Logan Pass.

The shuttle is a two-way service spanning Going-to-the-Sun Road from the Apgar Visitor Center to the St. Mary Visitor Center. The shuttle offers multiple stops on the west and east side of Logan Pass between the two visitor centers. On the west side from the Apgar Transit Center to Logan Pass, buses depart every 15-30 minutes. On the east side from the St. Mary Transit Center to Logan Pass, buses depart every 40 to 60 minutes.

McDonald Creek

There is an express shuttle service from the Apgar Visitor Center straight to Logan Pass at certain times of the day that is an option for those who are planning a hike from Logan Pass and want to get up there early, without having to stop at all of the shuttle stops.

The last departures from Logan Pass are at 7:00 p.m. to both the Apgar Visitor Center and the St. Mary Visitor Center. Do not miss these shuttles.

There is not a shuttle that goes straight from Apgar to St. Mary. You have to connect at Logan Pass and change shuttles to travel between these two points.

> Be prepared to be away from your vehicle for several hours, or possibly the entire day depending on your plans. You should bring a daypack with sufficient food, water, and extra clothing. You cannot get drinking water at every shuttle stop, so bring enough for the day. Spigots are available in most campgrounds. There are not restrooms at every stop. Pets are not allowed on the shuttle.

Because it is free, you do not need a ticket, and you can get on and off wherever you choose. Be prepared for shuttles to be crowded, and be ready to possibly wait for the

East side of Going-to-the-Sun Road

next one if the first is too full. If you lose an item on the bus, call (406) 888-7820 to see if it has been turned in.

This is not a tour service, so there is no commentary provided by the drivers.

For those traveling with children, car seats are not required on the shuttle. Strollers are welcome but must fit through the shuttle doors.

The shuttle is a popular choice for those hiking the Highline Trail between Logan Pass and the Loop. The shuttle allows you to catch a ride up to Logan Pass and hike back down to the Loop via the Highline Trail. While this is a great option for those wanting to hike the Highline Trail, this makes the Loop shuttle stop very popular, and limited seating is available.

> I personally struggle to use the shuttle with small children. Because we carry many items for our children, and we don't like to be on the shuttle schedule, I usually do not use the shuttle system.

For more information on the shuttle system, current schedule, and how to use the shuttle, visit **nps.gov/glac/planyourvisit/usingshuttle.htm**.

Ready to kayak on Lake McDonald

Winter Programs

From January to March, rangers offer free snowshoe tours departing from the Apgar Visitor Center on Saturdays and Sundays. Snowshoes can be rented for a nominal fee from the Apgar Visitor Center. These tours give you a look into Glacier National Park in the winter, while discussing wildlife and plants in the park. Dress in layers and bring water and snacks. The winter snowshoe tours are not recommended for children under the age of 6. I would not hesitate to do a tour with a small child in a backpack carrier. Call (406) 888-7800 for more information.

Horseback Riding

Swan Mountain Outfitters is the only company that offers horseback rides inside of Glacier National Park at Apgar, Many Glacier, and Lake McDonald. They also offer a trail ride that leaves from West Glacier, just outside of the West Entrance to Glacier National Park.

A trail ride is a wonderful activity for families. However, Swan Mountain Outfitters does not take kids under the age of 7 on trail rides. Children must be age 7 or over for the Apgar, Lake McDonald Lodge, and West Glacier corrals. Children must be age 8 or over for rides at the Many Glacier corral.

A wintery view from Apgar Lookout

Each location offers various ride lengths and options to fit your desires. Your wrangler will provide information about plants, animals, and the history of Glacier National Park depending on your location.

Tips For Your Horseback Ride

- Long pants and closed toed shoes are required.
- Bring a hat, sunscreen, and water.
- Dress in layers, mornings are cold in Montana. Even in the summer.
- 250 pounds is the weight limit, and they do have a scale there to check your weight. This is for the safety of the horses.
- The fee for the ride does not include gratuity for the wrangler, so be sure to tip them if you feel that you received good service.
- It may take a minimum of 45 minutes to check everyone in. If you want to know how long you should expect to be with Swan Mountain Outfitters, be sure to ask for each particular ride.

Ask for a pony ride

- *Helmets are provided; adults can choose whether they want to wear them, but children are required to wear them.*

Tip For Family With Young Children

If your child is too young to go on a trail ride, be sure to ask your outfitter if they will allow your child to go for a "pony ride." Although Swan Mountain does not actually have "ponies," they will allow small children to go on a horse ride around the corral with them leading the horse. This is a great free service, so that your small children are not left out of the fun. Be sure to tip the guide who takes the time to give your children a ride.

Swan Mountain Outfitters also offers multi-day Llama treks. Contact them for more information. Call (406) 387-4405, or (877) 888-5557 to make a reservation. Visit their website at **swanmountainoutfitters.com** for more information.

Payment is required in full to make a reservation in advance.

Trail riding near West Glacier

The Garden Wall reflected in McDonald Creek

Photo courtesy of Blake Passmore

Chapter Three: Going-to-the-Sun Road and Logan Pass

Going-to-the-Sun Road is a National Historic Landmark and is one of the main reasons people come to Glacier National Park. This road runs for 50 miles from Apgar to St. Mary, crossing over Logan Pass, offering incredible scenery and history. This road is the only way to connect from the west to the east side of Glacier National Park while remaining inside the Park.

Driving Going-to-the-Sun Road

Going-to-the-Sun Road, in its full length from the West Entrance to the East Entrance, is generally open from the end of June until the middle of September, but this depends completely on snow. Glacier National Park has to plow the roads in the early summer months to clear the snow before the road will open to vehicles. Be sure to check Glacier National Park's current road status page at **home.nps.gov/applications/glac/roadstatus/road-status.cfm**, to know if Going-to-the-Sun Road has opened in its entirety yet.

From the middle of September until the middle of October, you can usually drive from the West Entrance to Logan Pass, but not over the pass to St. Mary. This is always dependent on road construction and possible snowfall.

During the winter months, you can drive from the West Entrance to the Lake McDonald Lodge. On the east side of the Park, you can drive from the East Entrance to the foot of St. Mary Lake – about a mile and a half. If you plan to visit during the winter, be sure to visit the west side of the park at Lake McDonald. See Chapter ten for more information on visiting during the winter months.

If Going-to-the-Sun Road is not open over Logan Pass, you can use U.S. Highway 2 to drive around between West Glacier and East Glacier.

Without stopping, it will take you about 2 hours to drive Going-to-the-Sun Road in its entirety. However, you could easily spend an entire day driving the road from end to end. There are plenty of scenic pullouts to stop for pictures. There are several places along McDonald Creek that are worth stopping to enjoy. You will also want to stop at Logan Pass, and you can hike many places along Going-to-the-Sun Road if you want to take the time to see more than what is offered from the road.

Going-to-the-Sun Road is a very narrow two-lane road, particularly narrow on the west side of Logan Pass. Because the avalanches and snowfall destroys all protective barriers placed along Going-to-the-Sun Road, there are very few barriers in place. A small rock wall is placed along some parts of the road. This road may be frightening to drive for some, and for those, I would recommend taking a Red Bus Tour or the free shuttle service. Information on the Red Bus Tour and free shuttle can be found in Chapter Two.

View from Big Bend on Going-to-the-Sun Road

Vehicles and vehicle combinations (camper-trailers, RV's, etc.), longer than 21 feet or wider than 8 feet (including your mirrors) are prohibited over Logan Pass. This means you cannot drive them between Avalanche Campground and Rising Sun. If you have a vehicle longer than 21 feet, you will need to drive US Highway 2 between West Glacier and East Glacier to access opposite sides of the Park.

Vehicles that are higher than ten feet may not want to drive west from Logan Pass due to several rock overhangs.

Going-to-the-Sun Road is not open over Logan Pass during the winter months. Because of the tremendous amount of snowfall, this road is impossible to snowplow in the winter. The snowplowing is quite the event in the spring, as Glacier shares photos of its snowplows on their website as they work to open the road each year. You can see the snowplow progress at **nps.gov/glac**.

Haystack Creek on Going-to-the-Sun Road

You cannot get gas inside of Glacier Park, so be sure to fill up before you enter the Park. Food and lodging can be found inside of the park at Apgar Village, Lake McDonald Lodge, and Rising Sun, all found along Going-to-the-Sun Road.

If you want to see a glacier from the road, Jackson Glacier is visible from an overlook along Going-to-the-Sun Road on the east side between St. Mary and Logan Pass. There is a sign pointing to the turnout.

Logan Pass

Logan Pass

Logan Pass is located along the Continental Divide between St. Mary and West Glacier. This is the highest point of Going-to-the-Sun Road at 6,646 feet in elevation.

Wildlife at Logan Pass

Logan Pass is one of the best places in Glacier Park to get a close look at mountain goats and Bighorn sheep. Just past the turn-in to the Logan Pass Visitor Center up on the mountain to your left, there is often a group of Bighorn sheep. These sheep often wander down and around the parking lot, particularly later in the evening. Mountain goats are often seen around Logan Pass, particularly at the first pullout west of the Visitor Center. Mountain Goats can also be seen along the hike to the Hidden Lake Overlook and along the Highline Trail.

Logan Pass Visitor Center

The only attraction at Logan Pass – besides outstanding views and hiking - is the Logan Pass Visitor Center. The Visitor Center is a wonderful resource, providing an opportunity to speak to rangers and purchase guidebooks and gifts.

The Logan Pass parking lot is quite small for the amount of traffic it endures, and is usually full between 9:00 am and 4:00 p.m. during the busy season. Therefore, try to stop at the pass earlier in the morning or later in the evening. There is a sign on the road that will advise travelers if the parking lot has filled. Even if the sign says it is full, take a few laps around the lot and hope to find someone leaving. This pinnacle of Going-to-the-Sun Road should not be missed.

Logan Pass Visitor Center

There is the free shuttle service from the St. Mary Visitor Center or the Apgar Visitor Center that can take you to Logan Pass.

Read about the shuttle service in Chapter Two.

The Garden Wall from Logan Pass

Photo courtesy of Blake Passmore

Programs at Logan Pass

There are ranger-led programs offered in the Logan Pass area of the park for families to enjoy. Read more about what the Glacier National Park programs entail in Chapter Two. Glacier National Park often changes their programs, so be sure to check the current year's Ranger-Led Activity Schedule for the month you are visiting to check the available dates and times of each program listed here.

Hiking at Logan Pass

The hikes listed in this chapter begin from Logan Pass. There are a lot of family-friendly hikes that begin along Going-to-the-Sun Road, which you will find in the chapters covering Lake McDonald and St. Mary.

Hidden Lake Overlook

The Hidden Lake Overlook is a popular hike leaving from Logan Pass Visitor Center. This is one of the best hikes in Glacier National Park for families. You also have the option of continuing on to Hidden Lake (see below).

The Hidden Lake Overlook is 1.5 miles one-way, with an elevation gain of 460 feet, up to a lookout with beautiful views of Hidden Lake below. The hike begins as a paved trail, and then is mostly a raised boardwalk, and you will be joined by a lot of other people on this hike.

To get to the start of the trail, follow the path behind the Visitor Center, and continue on the path that heads toward Clements Mountain straight ahead of you. The trail is impossible to miss – just look for the boardwalk winding up the mountain.

Hiking to Hidden Lake

The views you get for most of the hike to the Hidden Lake Overlook are similar to what you see at Logan Pass. But the views from the Overlook itself are gorgeous, with Hidden Lake, Lake McDonald, and incredible mountains in view. You will also pass a pretty, small, unnamed lake to your left on your way up. Keep walking past it to the designated overlook for beautiful views.

This is a great hike with kids, because the hike is mostly on the boardwalk, fairly easy, and you are very likely to see mountain goats near the overlook.

Be sure to bring a hat and sunscreen on this hike. There is no shade and very few trees on this hike. There is also no bathroom. This spot can also get quite windy, so it's best to pack extra clothing. Also, if you do this hike early in the season (June / July), there is likely to be snow on the trail as you get closer to the overlook, so bring appropriate footwear. In the spring you will see people hiking up Clements Mountain and skiing down! Feel free to bring skis and join in the fun!

The open meadows you pass for the majority of the hike are referred to as the Hanging Gardens, and throughout the summer there are beautiful wildflowers blooming. Even if you don't complete the entire hike, you will enjoy walking the boardwalk and enjoying the vistas and wildflowers.

Hidden Lake Trail

The Hidden Lake Trail is one of my most favorite hikes in Glacier, because the lake itself is secluded, clear, and beautiful. You may be lucky enough to see a bear at the lake, so bring your bear spray!

This hike leaves from Logan Pass, and you will begin by hiking the 1.5 miles to the Hidden Lake Overlook. The elevation gain in this section is somewhere around 500 feet (different sources quote different elevation gain). Remember to arrive at Logan Pass early to get parking in the small lot!

You can see the entire trail down to the lake once you leave the Hidden Lake Overlook and continue the remaining 1.5 miles one-way down to the lake. This part of the hike is fairly steep and rocky, and drops around 500 feet down to the lake. Keep in mind that you have to turn around and hike out again. I would recommend only doing this hike with children who are stable on their feet.

Enjoying the shoreline of Hidden Lake

This hike is a fantastic place to see mountain goats and their cute kids!

If you head to your right once you reach the lake, you can follow the beach to your right to reach the outlet. You will follow a trail that runs parallel to the beach for a short way to reach the outlet. This is a gorgeous creek running away from the lake. If you continue to follow the trail that runs parallel to the lake, it will take you about 200 yards to a waterfall.

Right before the outlet on your left is the perfect spot for lunch. This spot gives you beach access, but also gives you some shade with the trees, which is hard to find on this beach that faces the sun.

There is a pit toilet at the lake. Bring a swimsuit if you want to take a dip in the cold lake.

Hidden Lake closes certain times of the year due to fish spawning and the bear activity because of the fish. Even if the trail to Hidden Lake is closed, the Hidden Lake Overlook is a gorgeous place to view Hidden Lake from above.

The Highline Trail

The Highline Trail is one of the most well-known and popular hikes in Glacier. Listed as the number one day hike in Hike 734's "Day Hikes of Glacier National Park," this is a spectacular hike for many reasons, but not one that should be done with small children.

This hike is popular because it is accessible directly from the Logan Pass parking lot, provides stunning panoramic views of Glacier, and is considered fairly easy because it has little elevation gain. The Highline follows the Continental Divide along what is called the Garden Wall, all of the way to the Granite Park Chalet.

Views on Highline Trail

The easiest way to do this hike is to park at the Loop, and catch the free shuttle up to Logan Pass. You will depart from Logan Pass and follow the trail until you reach the Granite Park Chalet, and then hike down from the chalet to the Loop, to pick up your vehicle. The total hike is over 11 miles, so you will want an entire day to complete this hike, depending on how often you hike.

For those looking for a shorter hike, you can hike from Logan Pass for about three and a half miles to Haystack Butte, which is a nice place to stop for lunch before returning to Logan Pass. For this version of the hike, park in the Visitor Center parking lot, and look for the trailhead across Going-to-the-Sun Road.

Near the beginning of the trail, you will find the "Rimrock" section of the hike where the trail is only about four feet wide and there is a sheer cliff to one side that drops

The Rimrock Section on the Highline Trail

about a hundred feet onto Going-to-the-Sun Road. During the summer months there is a cable handrail along this section. The cable is removed for the winter months each September.

The cliff section is the worst part of it, but most of this hike is a trail that is not very wide that is cut into the side of the mountain, providing steep drops to one side. This is not the hike for you if you are afraid of heights or are not stable on your feet. In my opinion, this is not a safe hike for toddlers or small children. We have carried our children in backpacks on this hike, but will not do so again for several years. We even saw one woman frozen with fear turn back halfway through the cliff section. This trail is not very wide and is precarious for unstable or acrophobic hikers.

> Warnings aside, I agree with Jake Bramante's opinion that this is Glacier's best "bang for your buck" hike – fairly easy, with stunning views. If you have a day, this is a hike that is easily accessible from Going-to-the-Sun Road, and will provide you with stunning views of Glacier National Park.

Bicycles on Going-to-the-Sun Road

Bicycles are permitted on Going-to-the-Sun Road, but only during limited hours. Be sure to check ahead for the current hours that bikes are allowed. Bikes are usually allowed early in the morning and later in the evening. This is for everyone's safety, because the road is extremely narrow and there is a lot of traffic. Helmets are not required, but are strongly advised.

Glacier National Park estimates it will take you about 45 minutes to ride from Sprague Creek to Logan Creek, and about three hours to get from Logan Creek to Logan Pass, so be sure to start early.

During the spring and fall, when the road is closed to vehicle traffic, bicycles are allowed past Lake McDonald Lodge and Avalanche Creek to ride Going-to-the-Sun Road any time of day.

Dining

There is no food available at Logan Pass. Food is available in St. Mary and Rising Sun on the east side of the park, and food is available at Lake McDonald Lodge and Apgar on the west side of the park.

Avalanche Lake

Chapter Four: West Glacier, Apgar, and Lake McDonald

Going-to-the-Sun Road begins in West Glacier, traveling along Apgar and Lake McDonald, making nearly certain that you will travel through here. This entire area is often referred to as the Lake McDonald Valley. Besides the amazing views, this area offers camping, lodging, lake activities and hiking. This part of the park is a must-do for anyone visiting Glacier National Park.

West Glacier is located at the West Entrance to Glacier Park. This is a popular place to stay, for its proximity to Glacier International Airport and Lake McDonald. Lake McDonald is the largest lake in Glacier, at ten miles long and over a mile wide. Lake McDonald begins two miles from the West Entrance at Apgar Village, and is probably the most famous lake in the entire park.

West Glacier offers camping, lodging, fuel stations, groceries, laundromat, and a bar. There are gift shops and a few restaurants. Whitewater rafting, fishing, and scenic floats are available on the Middle Fork of the Flathead River, which flows right through town.

There is a train stop for the Amtrak station in West Glacier that has an enclosed waiting area and restrooms. West Glacier also is home to an Alberta Visitor Information Center that is open from May to mid-September. The Center is located at the intersection of Highway 2 and Going-to-the-Sun Road. This center is dedicated to helping you plan your trip in Canada once you cross the border, and is a great place to stop to explore cool exhibits, including a T-Rex display in the lobby. They have interesting information available, and restrooms open to the public.

Apgar is a small village just inside the park entrance along the southern shore of Lake McDonald. The views from Apgar are what welcome most visitors into the park. Apgar has a Visitor Center, the Apgar Campground, the Apgar Nature Center, a few hotels, and a small grocery store. You can purchase firewood in Apgar.

Sunrise over the Middle Fork of the Flathead River

There are boat rentals available in Apgar, but there are no tours of Lake McDonald departing from here – you need to travel to the Lake McDonald Lodge for those.

Ten miles of driving from Apgar along Going-to-the-Sun Road will take you to the Lake McDonald Lodge. Going-to-the-Sun Road follows the shore of Lake McDonald the entire way, offering plenty of areas to pull out and take photos or enjoy some time by the lake. These are some of my favorite beaches on Lake McDonald.

The Lake McDonald Lodge offers limited amenities, including an ATM, gift shop, a campstore, and a few places to eat.

Hiking

Hiking in the Apgar and Lake McDonald area is popular because a lot of people stay on the west side of the Park, and there are many easier, family-friendly trails available here.

McDonald Creek

Trail of the Cedars (stroller/wheelchair accessible)

The Trail of the Cedars is an easy, wheelchair-accessible family stroll. You will walk on a raised boardwalk through the western hemlock and red cedars for a one-mile loop. I would not call this so much a hike, as more of a nice walk through the old forest.

At about halfway, you will get to see the beautiful Avalanche Gorge with the waterfall flowing between two mossy cliffs. This is a great photo opportunity, and there is no reason that everyone should not see this on a trip to Glacier. Just beyond Avalanche Gorge (if walking the loop clockwise), you can turn to hike up to Avalanche Lake, or keep following the path back to your vehicle.

The Trail of the Cedars
Photo courtesy of Blake Passmore

Avalanche Lake

The Avalanche Lake hike is one of the most popular in the park, and for good reason. You park right along Going-to-the-Sun Road between Lake McDonald and Logan Pass, and the hike is a 4 and a half-mile round-trip hike to an alpine lake with waterfalls cascading into it.

The trail begins from Trail of the Cedars taking you by the Avalanche Gorge and along the Avalanche Creek through the old growth forest. Large rocks, moss, and the water make this feel like something from the *Lord of the Rings*. There are a few small hills to

climb throughout the hike, with an elevation gain of about 500 feet. The lake is worth the trip and you will want to set aside some time to enjoy the scenery at the lake and sit on the beach with a snack. The aggressive chipmunks will have no problem stealing your lunch - do not let them!

Keep in mind the waterfalls are larger earlier in the season when the snow is still melting. This is a popular hike, and parking can be impossible to find. This is a great hike to do earlier or later in the day, as it is packed in the middle of the afternoon. I recommend arriving before 9 a.m. or after 3 p.m. to begin your hike. Add Avalanche Lake to your list!

In early summer, the shores of Avalanche Lake are a great place to see black bears.

Avalanche Lake

Johns Lake Loop

Johns Lake Loop is an easy hike for families with kids of all ages. This trail will take you through a beautiful forest of hemlock trees, past muddy Johns Lake, along McDonald Creek and McDonald Falls, and back to your vehicle. The hike is a 1.8-mile loop that begins at the Johns Lake trailhead just over a mile east of the Lake McDonald Lodge on Going-to-the-Sun Road.

You will begin by following the trail into the woods (do not cross over the Going-to-the-Sun at this time). There are a few junctions you will need to follow, but there are easy signs showing you that at the first junction you will turn left, and at the second junction you will turn right. You will soon reach Johns Lake, which is more of a boggy pond with gorgeous reflections of Stanton Mountain and Mount Vaught.

Keep hiking past Johns Lake, soon emerging from the forest and crossing Going-to-the-Sun Road, where you will cross over McDonald Creek on the bridge below Sacred Dancing Cascade and turn left to follow the beautiful trail along the creek, passing McDonald Falls before you reach North McDonald Lake Road. At one point along the creek, you will pass a small log bench and there will be a fork, and you want to stay to the left. Once you reach North McDonald Lake Road, turn left and cross the bridge. Crossing over North McDonald Lake Road after the bridge will take you to the trail that will lead you back to your vehicle on Going-to-the-Sun Road.

There is only room for about 8 cars at the trailhead, so I would recommend arriving before 9:30 a.m. to guarantee a spot to park.

Johns Lake

Forest and Fire Nature Trail

The Forest and Fire Nature Trail is a nice hike for families because it is short and easy. Round-trip the trail is only 1.1 miles, making it more of a leisurely stroll. The trail leads you through the lodge pole pine forest that with surrounding dead trees showing the damage from a fire in 1967 and the Moose Fire in 2001.

This trail may still be marked as the Huckleberry Mountain Nature Trail, although it has since been renamed.

Hiking near West Glacier

The trail begins near the Camas Road Entrance to the Park near the North Fork. Look for the sign pointing you up a short side road to take you up the hill to a small parking lot where the trail begins.

While this hike is a pretty walk through the trees, the view into the North Fork is one you can get simply by driving up the side road to the parking lot. If you want to hike to bigger views and lakes, skip this one.

Rocky Point Nature Trail

The hike to Rocky Point on the west shore of Lake McDonald is an easy, pretty hike that gives you access to isolated beaches and rewards you with alternative views of the lake, Apgar and the surrounding mountains. There are a few minor hills to hike, but this easy hike is only 1.9 miles round-trip.

To reach the trailhead, drive along Camas Road until you reach the turn on your right toward Fish Creek Campground. Just over a mile down the road you will reach a fork, and you will turn left onto the Inside North Fork Road instead of right into the campground. Take the gravel North Fork Road for about a half of a mile until you see the sign on your right for the Rocky Point trailhead and just past that on your left is a small parking lot. Park in the parking lot and walk back down the road to start at the trailhead.

You will cross over Fern Creek, then hike over a hill and come to a fork where you will stay to the left to head toward Rocky Point. Turning right will take you to some nice sandier beaches by the Fish Creek Campground.

When you reach the next fork, you will stay to the right; this is the loop that is the Rocky Point Nature Trail. Shortly after this you reach a small fork where it says to stay straight (or to the left) to stay on Rocky Point Trail. However, if you turn to the right, the trail takes you down a very short distance to Rocky Point and to gorgeous rocky beaches facing Apgar that you will likely have all to yourself.

The beach at Rocky Point

Head back up to the main trail from the far end of your detour trail and continue along through the forest, where you will see the destruction caused by the 2003 Robert Fire that burned more than 136,000 acres in Glacier. This opens up the view for you to see the head of Lake McDonald. You will then reach the Lake McDonald Trail Junction, and take a left to get back to the trail where you began and to the parking lot.

Stanton Lake

Stanton Lake is a pretty lake found between East Glacier and West Glacier on Highway 2. While this lake is not inside of Glacier National Park, it is worth mentioning because it is pretty short and beautiful. It has also remained fairly undiscovered (relative to the hikes inside the park), making it a great place to avoid crowds.

Stanton Lake
Photo courtesy of Blake Passmore

This hike is somewhere between three and four miles round-trip, depending on what source you ask. Some sources report this hike to be flat and easy; it is not flat. There is a steep hill you must climb, and then you drop a little downhill to get to the lake. So you must climb back up that hill to get back out.

Bring your dog and horse, and enjoy this hike! Drive through West Glacier toward East Glacier, and take your first right past the Stanton Lodge between mile markers 169 and 170. Park in the parking lot and follow the trail.

Programs

There are several programs offered in this area of Glacier National Park for families to enjoy. Read more about what the Glacier National Park programs entail in *Chapter Two*. Glacier often changes its programs, so be sure to check the current year's Ranger-Led Activity Schedule for the month you are visiting to check the available dates and times of each program.

Drop-in Programs

Glacier National Park offers drop-in programs where a ranger is available to discuss specific topics in a certain location. One of these is the Apgar Nature Center, a cabin in the woods in Apgar that provides an opportunity for children to learn about wildlife and nature. *You can read more about the Apgar Nature Center in the Ranger-Led Activity Chapter.*

Check the Ranger-Led Activity Schedule for current drop-in programs available in the Lake McDonald Valley during the month of your visit.

Lake McDonald from Apgar Lookout

Self-Guided Walking Tour of the Park Headquarters

The Park Headquarters are located near West Glacier, Montana, just inside the West Entrance. The park headquarters historic district is listed in the National Register of Historic Places, and you can do a self-guided walking tour of the headquarters. The tour is about a mile long and will take you about one hour, depending on how fast or slow you choose to go. Call (406) 281-7023 from any cell phone to learn about the architecture and history of the building as you go, or download a tour brochure from the National Park Service website for Glacier National Park.

Boat Rentals

Boat rentals are available from the Glacier Park Boat Company at Apgar, including rowboats, paddleboards, canoes, single and double kayaks, and 8 hp and 10hp motorboats.

There are also other companies in Apgar that rent paddleboards. They rent them from two hours up to overnight.

At Lake McDonald Lodge, the Glacier Park Boat Company offers rowboats and motorboats for rent throughout the summer.

Paddleboards can be rented at Apgar

Call (406) 257-2426 to reach the Glacier Park Boat Company for information.

Boat Tours

Boat tours are not available leaving from Apgar. You must travel to the Lake McDonald Lodge for the boat tours of Lake McDonald. The Lake McDonald Boat Tour departs from the Lake McDonald Lodge Boat Dock, taking you on a one-hour tour aboard the historic *DeSmet* boat to hear about this area and Glacier's stories. You can buy tickets at the boat dock, or call 406-257-2426 to make reservations.

Same day reservations are accepted at Lake McDonald. I would recommend reservations, as these tours do fill quickly. Arrive 15 minutes prior to departure.

Fall in Glacier

Children's Programs

Children's Programs are specifically tailored for families and children, and adults must attend with children. Glacier National Park offers a few choices of children's programs in the Lake McDonald Valley.

I highly recommend participating in one or more of these programs if you are traveling with children.

Ranger-Led Walks and Hikes

The Lake McDonald Valley has several ranger-led walks available throughout the summer. These programs are free of charge. Be sure to check the Ranger-Led Activity Schedule to see the current programs available during your visit.

See the T-Rex at the Alberta Visitor Center in West Glacier

Talks and Evening Programs

There are evening programs available at the Lake McDonald Lodge, the Apgar Campground Amphitheater, and the Fish Creek Campground Amphitheater. Non-campers are welcome at the campground programs, and there is limited parking available. There are ranger talks available at the Apgar Nature Center. The McDonald Valley also offers the Native America Speaks series. Check the Ranger-Led Activity Schedule for current programs and the schedule for the month you are visiting.

Camping

There are plenty of options for camping on the west side of Glacier. Some campgrounds offer campsites directly on Lake McDonald, and others are near it.

For general information about camping inside of Glacier National Park, see Chapter Two.

Apgar Campground

The Apgar Campground is the largest campground in Glacier, with 194 campsites available. While the campground is not located directly on Lake McDonald, it is only a short walk to the lake from any of the campsites. The campground has both tent and RV camper sites, and potable water is accessible in the campground. Their restroom facilities provide flush toilets and sinks with running water, but there are no showers available. There is also a dump station. All sites have a fire ring and a picnic table.

Getting up early (top) and going to bed late (lower) can be rewarding at Apgar.

Photos courtesy of Blake Passmore

The Apgar Campground is first-come first-serve; so the earlier you arrive in the day, the better your chances of getting a spot. This campground will fill daily during the summer. Loop A is the most desirable because it has large sites and is the closest to Lake McDonald. However, all of the campsites at Apgar Campground are large and comfortable. There are also a few walk-up sites that are less expensive for those traveling without a vehicle.

Reservations are accepted for the group sites up to 12 months in advance, which can be made at **Recreation.gov**. Group sites are for 9 or more campers. The group site reservations must be made at least 3 days in advance, and remember that there are no refunds so be sure to only pay for the nights you are sure you will be staying.

The summer season here runs from the beginning of May until around the second week in October. Primitive camping is available other times of the year for a smaller nightly fee. Winter camping is available from December to March for no charge. During primitive camping and winter camping at Apgar, the campground is closed but you can camp at the picnic area across the road from the campground. There will not be water available during primitive and winter camping, so you will need to bring your own drinking water.

This campground is not located directly on Lake McDonald, but is only a short walk from the lake in the trees. The trees provide every camping site with plenty of shade from the heat in the middle of summer. This makes it a wonderful place for families to stay, as you are only a very short walk down to the beach. An evening sunset at Lake McDonald is not to be missed during your trip to Glacier National Park.

Avalanche Creek
Photo courtesy of Blake Passmore

There is a flat, paved walking path from the Apgar Campground leading to the Apgar Visitor Center and to Apgar Village. Apgar has a small grocery store and restaurant called Eddie's as well as boat rentals. From the Visitor Center, you can catch a Red Bus tour or use the free shuttle service to take you along Going-to-the-Sun Road.

Apgar Campground also offers evening programs at the Apgar Amphitheater with a park ranger. Check the Ranger-led Activity Schedule for times. You can find the Activity Schedule at the Apgar Visitor Center, the West Entrance, or at the small covered cabin located just inside the campground on an outdoor table. The topics vary, so be sure to check the bulletin board posted at the amphitheater to view the topics.

As long as you arrive early in the day, you will surely find a spot, as this campground tends to fill later in the day than some other campgrounds in the Park. There is so much to see and do in the Apgar and Lake McDonald area, and using this campground as your base is an affordable and fun option.

Avalanche Campground

Avalanche Campground sits nearly 16 miles from the West Entrance, past Lake McDonald. This is a popular campground because it is located at the start of the Trail of the Cedars and Avalanche Lake hikes, and is the closest campground on the west side to Logan Pass. Since it is first-come, first-serve, you need to arrive early in the day to get a camping spot here.

Avalanche Campground has 87 campsites available, with 50 of those sites accommodating up to a 26-foot RV or truck and trailer combination. Potable water is available in the campground, and restrooms have flush toilets and running water.

Avalanche Campground does not operate in a primitive status, and thus is only open

Enjoying the shore of Lake McDonald

during the summer season from the middle of June to the middle of September.

The free shuttle service stops at Avalanche Campground, making it easy to catch a shuttle to Logan Pass. Be sure to catch an evening program with a Park Ranger at the Avalanche Amphitheater during your stay.

Avalanche Creek is beautiful, with the famous Avalanche Gorge cascading down into the creek along the Trail of the Cedars.

Fish Creek Campground (accepts reservations)

Fish Creek Campground is one of the most popular campgrounds in the park. Fish Creek is the second largest campground in Glacier with 178 campsites, and is one of only two campgrounds that accept reservations. This campground is located just off of the Camas Road, about 2.5 miles west of Apgar Village and is on the southwest shore of Lake McDonald. Some of the campsites are on Lake McDonald.

This is one of the few campgrounds that have a shower available. Showers are located in Loop A, and are only for registered campers. Potable water is available, and bathrooms provide flush toilets and sinks with running water.

The Fish Creek Campground is located in the trees, providing plenty of shade at every campsite. Loop D is my favorite loop, with some of these sites having views and access to Lake McDonald right from the campsite. Loop C is my least favorite loop, with a lot of the campsites on hillsides that don't give campers much space, especially if you have children that need room to move. Note that Loop C in the Fish Creek Campground is generator-free. A free ranger-led program is presented in the amphitheater each evening.

Kayaking near Fish Creek

Fish Creek Campground is open from early June to early September. Reservations can be made at **recreation.gov** and can be made up to 6 months in advance of your arrival date. Reservations are required to be made three days in advance. Any sites that are not reserved ahead of time will be available upon your arrival on a first-come, first-serve basis. You can check the Campground Status page on Glacier National Park's website to check whether there are still sites available.

Sprague Creek Campground (tent only)

Sprague Creek Campground is a small campground located on the northeast shores of Lake McDonald with 25 campsites available. The campground is located in the trees and is tent camping only. This campground is first-come, first-serve, and I would recommend you arrive early because it fills quickly.

All of the campsites are right on Lake McDonald, requiring only a short walk to the lake. Here you will find quiet because Sprague Creek is a generator-free campground and no towed units are allowed, but since the campground is located directly on Going-to-the-Sun Road, you will have noise from the traffic driving by.

Sprague Creek is open from early May to mid-September, and will cost you $20.00 per night. Potable water is accessible, and restrooms have running water and flush toilets. There are no showers here. If you need any amenities, the Lake McDonald Lodge is only a mile from the campground up Going-to-the-Sun Road, where you can find a camp store, a restaurant, and a gift shop. The Lake McDonald Lodge also offers boat tours, and horseback riding.

View of shoreline of Lake McDonald at Sprague Creek Campground
Photo courtesy of Blake Passmore

The free shuttle service provided by Glacier National Park stops at the pull-off on Going-to-the-Sun Road, directly across from the Sprague Creek Campground.

Sprague Creek is a pretty campground, and popular for its location on Lake McDonald. If you are looking for a family spot and you are traveling with a tent, this is the place for you.

Hotels

There are only a few choices of lodging in Apgar Village and along Lake McDonald. These include the Village Inn and the Apgar Village Lodge in Apgar Village at the southern end of Lake McDonald. The Lake McDonald Lodge and the Motel Lake McDonald are on the eastern shore of Lake McDonald closer to Logan Pass. Keep in mind that lodging inside of the park can all be considered quite rustic.

There are also several choices for lodging and campgrounds outside of Glacier in nearby West Glacier, Lake Five, and Hungry Horse.

> Where you stay on the west side of the park is a matter of personal preference. For traveling around Glacier, and to get the authentic Glacier National Park experience, I would suggest staying as close to the Park as possible. This means staying in West Glacier, Apgar, or Lake McDonald. In order to get reservations in these places, you need to book in advance. I recommend reserving accommodations 6 months ahead of time.

A portion of the Lake McDonald Lodge accommodations.

Photo courtesy of Blake Passmore

Picnic Spots

Avalanche Creek

Avalanche Creek is absolutely stunning. Avalanche Gorge flows into Avalanche Creek and runs down into McDonald Creek. There is a large rocky beach where the two creeks meet, near the parking area for the Trail of the Cedars and Avalanche Lake hikes. I love this spot for a picnic. The blue water and surrounding peaks from this spot are incredible. You can't see this beach from the road, but there are plenty of day use spots here with picnic tables and fire rings, and this beach is one of my favorite spots on the west side of the Park.

Sprague Creek Campground

Sprague Creek Campground along Lake McDonald also has several spots that are reserved for day use picnics. This campground has a nice beach looking toward the peaks at the head of Lake McDonald. The picnic spots are large and provide picnic tables and fire rings. Even if you don't camp here, swing in and have a picnic and enjoy the beach.

Lake McDonald Lodge

Fish Creek Picnic Area

There is a picnic area just before the Fish Creek Campground that has a large beach area on Lake McDonald with picnic tables and some shade. This is a spectacular beach and will be less crowded than the shores of Lake McDonald near Apgar Village. This is my favorite beach in the mornings before the sun gets too hot, as it faces into the morning sun, making it nice and warm for breakfast at a picnic table and a morning swim.

Lake McDonald Pullouts

There are 11 pullouts along Lake McDonald's shores between the turn to Apgar Campground and the Lake McDonald Lodge. This is not including Sprague Creek Campground.

Some of the pullouts along Lake McDonald offer better views and better beaches than others. As the water level drops later in the summer and fall, most of the stops offer larger and nicer beaches. A few of the pullouts have garbage cans.

Our favorite spot to pull over is the fifth pullout past the turn to Apgar as you head toward the Lake McDonald Lodge. A large beach offers views toward Apgar and toward the head of Lake McDonald and Logan Pass.

Flinsch Peak from the summit of Rising Wolf Mountain

Photo courtesy of Blake Passmore

Chapter Five:
East Glacier and Two Medicine

East Glacier is a small town located at the southeastern corner of Glacier National Park that provides access to the Two Medicine area and Two Medicine Entrance to the park. As mentioned previously, the town of East Glacier is actually about an hour drive from the St. Mary Entrance (where Going-to-the-Sun Road begins). East Glacier is home to the stunning Glacier Park Lodge, a 9-hole golf course, a few restaurants, gas stations, gift shops, motels, and minimal groceries. You will not find nightlife, banks, pharmacies, or fast food.

My advice with East Glacier would be to use it as a base to access Two Medicine, one of my favorite regions. Otherwise, East Glacier is quite far from most of the major sites in the park.

Two Medicine is one of my favorite and one of the most stunning places in Glacier. The seclusion and surprising beauty add to the charm. Two Medicine has its own entrance into the park, and will take you about 20 minutes driving from East Glacier.

There is not much at Two Medicine except a campground, a ranger station, and a small camp store that sells snacks and drinks, soft serve ice cream, some camping gear, and gifts. There is not a restaurant here. There are boat tours and Red Bus tours available. While it is worth the drive even if you do nothing more than stop by the easy walk to Running Eagle Falls and take pictures of Two Medicine Lake, this area also has several family-friendly hiking opportunities.

Highway 49 is the highway that connects East Glacier to St. Mary. This is the highway you will use to get to Two Medicine. This scenic highway offers beautiful views of the eastern front of Glacier Park, while simultaneously offering views of the plains to the east. If you are pulling a camper trailer, you may want to drive around through Browning, as long vehicles are not recommended on this road. Highway 49 is approximately 13 miles from East Glacier to the junction of Highway 89 to turn to St. Mary.

There is no cell service in the Two Medicine Valley. There are no pay phones available at Two Medicine Lake. You will have cell service a few miles outside of the Two Medicine Entrance to Glacier Park. You will also have cell service in East Glacier.

Morning light on Pray Lake

Hiking

There are plenty of scenic hiking opportunities that are appropriate for families. Keep in mind that this is not an all-inclusive list of hikes, but rather a good list of hikes for families in this area.

Running Eagle Falls (stroller/wheelchair accessible)

If you visit the Two Medicine area, you will want to stop at Running Eagle Falls. Running Eagle Falls is a beautiful waterfall that is just past the Two Medicine entrance inside of Glacier Park. This waterfall is wheelchair and stroller accessible, as it is a wide, flat path that is only 0.3 miles one way. For those wanting to get a little closer, you can cross the footbridge and walk to the viewing platform.

Also known as "Trick Falls," the waterfall looks different depending on what time of year you visit. In the spring, the spring runoff causes the water to fall from the top, covering the lower waterfall

Running Eagle Falls

that comes through the rock. When the water level decreases later in the summer, the upper waterfall will disappear and you will only see the lower waterfall rushing through the rock in the cliff face. On a nice day, you may see people jumping off the rocks into the pool at the base of the falls.

Paradise Point

Paradise Point isn't so much a hike, as a nice place for a picnic stroll in the Two Medicine Valley. To get to Paradise Point, you will start at the South Shore Trailhead on Two Medicine Lake behind the ticket office for the boat tours. Not long after you reach the top of the hill, you will see a sign to your right pointing to Paradise Point. Follow that trail down through the trees and a small meadow until you reach the lake.

The round-trip length of this hike is 1.4 miles, and you will find a nice rocky beach on the shores of Two Medicine Lake that offers views looking to the head of the lake and back to the parking area and camp store. If you are brave enough to swim in the icy water, this is a good spot for it.

Aster Falls / Aster Park Overlook

The hike to Aster Falls is a mostly level, short hike. This hike begins from the South Shore Trailhead at Two Medicine Lake behind the ticket office for the boat tours. Except for one hill at the start, the hike is a level trail that goes through open meadows with gorgeous views of surrounding mountains.

Take a detour to Paradise Point, which will add a little more than a half-mile to your trip. You will see the sign not far from the start of your hike to get down to Paradise Point. This is a beach on Two Medicine Lake that offers a nice place for lunch and swimming if you can brave the cold water.

Aster Falls is a pretty waterfall, and at a round-trip length of 2.8 miles, is doable for kids of all ages. If your kids are a little older, continue on the trail to head up to the Aster Park Overlook.

The Aster Park Overlook hike is 4 miles round-trip, with over a 500-foot elevation gain. To get here, you will hike to Aster Falls, and then follow the trail heading up the hill. Several switchbacks later, mostly through the trees, will take you up a fairly steady climb to a nice open spot on the mountain with panoramic views of Aster Park and Two Medicine Lake. I found this view to be pretty and worth the hike, but just stopping at Aster Falls is fun as well.

Aster Falls

If you skip the Aster Park Overlook, you can see Aster Falls and keep hiking to Rockwell Falls.

Rockwell Falls

Rockwell Falls is a very pleasant, mostly level 7-mile hike round trip, with an elevation gain of approximately 375 feet. The hike starts by the boat dock on Two Medicine Lake, at the South Shore Trailhead. The trail begins by taking you up a small hill (this is really the only hill you will find on this hike). The trail then flattens and remains fairly flat the rest of the hike.

A lot of the hike is in the trees, but there are some places where it opens up and you get sweeping views of the surrounding mountains. There is also a fun swinging bridge, and a lot of huckleberries as you get closer to the waterfall. Bring a bag for taking huckleberries home with you.

Upper section of Rockwell Falls

Not far from the waterfall is a fork with an option of either hiking back around the lake the way you came, or hiking to the western shore boat dock and taking the Glacier Park Boat Company boat back for a fee. Keep in mind that the boat only picks up at this dock at specific times.

Rockwell Falls has several layers of waterfalls. You can sit at the bottom of the falls, or hike up and around and there are nice spots to sit and enjoy the water.

The trail continues on to Cobalt Lake and Two Medicine Pass if you wish to keep going, but I only recommend these longer trails for families with older children.

Twin Falls

The hike to Twin Falls is a gentle walk if you take a boat to get there. This is a great, flat family hike and the waterfalls are beautiful. Take any of the boat trips across Two Medicine Lake, and then get off and follow the signs to Twin Falls for a flat walk of about a mile each way. The hike takes you through the forest until you get to the two waterfalls flowing down a hillside about twenty yards apart. If you hike up the waterfall to the right, you will find a hidden swimming hole.

Twin Falls, left fork

If you take the boat, it is only about a mile each way on this enjoyable trail. Taking the boat will shave off nearly five or six miles round-trip (as there are two trails around the lake). Be sure to check what times the boat picks up and catch the boat back across the lake after you visit the waterfalls. You can always hike around Two Medicine Lake via the North Shore Trail if you miss the boat, but catching the boat is quicker and easier. The North Shore trail offers open views of Two Medicine Lake, and is mostly pretty level.

You can keep hiking past Twin Falls to Upper Two Medicine Lake.

Swimming hole at Twin Falls, right fork

Upper Two Medicine Lake

Upper Two Medicine Lake is an easy, pretty hike if you take the boat. For families making this trek, I advise you take the boat tour across Two Medicine Lake and begin hiking from there. If you take the boat, the hike is less than 2 ½ miles each way, and the elevation gain is minimal, around 300 feet.

The trail takes you through the forest, and you will pass by the short detour to Twin Falls, which I highly recommend. Toward the end of the trail, you emerge from the trees and the view opens up with 360-degree views of the surrounding mountains. The lake itself is pretty, but does not have much beach access. There is one little spot on the lake and a nice area with log seating back in the forest for enjoying lunch.

Upper Two Medicine Lake also has backcountry camping available. If your family is up to it, pack a tent and camping gear, and obtain a backcountry permit from the Two Medicine Ranger Station. Back country campsites can now be reserved in advance, read more about backcountry camping in Chapter Eleven.

Upper Two Medicine Lake

Be sure to check the times the boat will pick up to ensure you are back in time to catch the boat. If you do miss the last boat of the day, there is a trail leading around each side of Two Medicine Lake that allows you to hike back. The North Shore Trailhead leading to your left will take you to the Two Medicine Campground, and the South Shore Trailhead leading to your right will take you to the camp store and parking area.

Scenic Point

Scenic Point is a beautiful overlook with views of Two Medicine Lake and the surrounding mountains. This hike is 8 miles round-trip according to **hikinginglacier.com**, with an elevation gain of 2300 feet.

This is a popular hike because of the incredible views of the mountains and plains from the top. It is significant elevation gain for small children, and the top is known to be extremely windy and cold. So it is up to you to determine if this is a hike for you if you have small children. Otherwise, the views are definitely worth the hike!

The trailhead is found at the small parking lot to your left before you reach the turn into the Two Medicine Campground. Follow the signs to Scenic Point.

Appistoki Falls

Appistoki Falls is an easy hike to a waterfall that I would only spend time doing if you have extra time while visiting the Two Medicine Valley. This is an easy walk through the forest taking you to a viewing point of the waterfalls. The trail does not get up close to the waterfall. Park at the Scenic Point parking lot on your left before you reach the turn to the campground and follow the signs for a 0.6-mile walk each way.

Above an inversion on the Scenic Point Trail

Programs

There are several programs and activities offered in Two Medicine and East Glacier to enjoy. Read more about what the Glacier National Park programs entail in *Chapter Two*. Be sure to check the current year's Ranger-Led Activity Schedule for the month you are visiting to check the current programs, and available dates and times.

Boat Rentals

The Glacier Park Boat Company offers rowboats, canoes, and kayaks for rent from the boat dock at Two Medicine Lake. A rental boat is a great way to explore the lake and fish on your own.

Boat Tours

The Glacier Park Boat Company offers 45-minute boat tours on Two Medicine Lake five times a day throughout the summer. I prefer to catch the earliest boat trip if I plan on hiking and

The *Sinopah* and Sinopah Mountain on Two Medicine Lake

Kayak on Pray Lake at Two Medicine

catching a boat back. Parking is conveniently next to the boat dock. Certain tours also include an optional 2.5-hour, 2-mile round-trip guided hike to Twin Falls at no charge. If you don't wish to take the guided hike or a hike on your own, you can just return on the boat back to the main dock.

Children under age 4 are free. You can make a reservation by calling (406) 257-2426, keeping in mind that cell service is limited in this area. Remember that reservations must be made at least one day in advance for Two Medicine. Of course you can always show up and hope that there will be seats available at the time you wish to tour.

Be sure to pack your own food and beverage, as none are sold on the boat. There are also no bathrooms on the boat.

A boat tour is a fun way to see Two Medicine Lake, learn about the local history, and ask questions of your guide. The boat tour is also a great way to shave time and distance off of hikes in this area, including Twin Falls, Upper Two Medicine Lake, No Name Lake, and Dawson Pass.

If you are planning on hiking when you get to the other side of Two Medicine Lake, be sure to check the boat pickup times to ensure you catch the boat back on time. You will be given a return ticket to catch a later boat. The afternoon boats will do multiple trips if necessary to make sure that no hikers are left behind.

You can buy one-way boat trip tickets, and you can pay for your one-way boat trip back to the main dock after your boat ride. This allows you to hike one-way, and then if you decide not to hike back, you can catch a boat ride back.

For more information on boat tours and boat rentals, call (406) 257-2426, or visit glacierparkboats.com.

Ranger-Led Walks and Hikes in the Two Medicine Valley

Keep in mind that the walks and hikes listed here are always available to do on your own, without a ranger to guide you. There are pros and cons to hiking with a ranger that you can read about in *Chapter Two*. You will want to consider these before deciding whether to participate in a ranger-led hike. There are more ranger-led hikes available than I have listed here, but I did not list the difficult hikes that may not be the best idea if you have younger children or aren't in great shape.

The following list are examples of hikes that Glacier National Park has offered in prior years. These are subject to change at any time, so be sure to check the Ranger-Led Activity Schedule to see what is offered for the month and time you are visiting.

South Shore Trail

Aster Park Hike

The Aster Park Hike takes you to Aster Falls, and then up to the Aster Park Overlook with views of the Two Medicine Valley. Meet at the Two Medicine Campstore. Plan on 4 hours for the 3.8-mile (round-trip) hike with a 670-foot elevation gain. The hike to the falls is easy with kids, but the last part of the hike to the Overlook is where it climbs. The views are beautiful, but you will want to decide if your kids are up to the last switchback section.

Paradise Point Bird Walk

Meet at the Two Medicine Campstore for an easy 2-mile walk in the morning to see and listen to the birds in the Two Medicine Valley. Binoculars and a field guild are recommended. Expect this to take just under 2 hours.

Rockwell Falls

Rockwell Falls Hike

Rockwell Falls is a great, moderate hike with kids. You will hike to Aster Falls, and then continue until you reach the beautiful Rockwell Falls. Plan on 5 hours for this 6.8-mile hike. Meet at the Two Medicine Campstore.

Boat Tours with a Hike

There are a few boat tours that offer a ranger-led hike. Keep in mind you still have to pay for the boat tour, but the ranger-led hiking part is free. You can take the boat tour at any of the offered times throughout the day, but a few of the offered times will also offer a hike led by a ranger. There are ranger-led hikes with the boat tour to No Name Lake, Dawson Pass, and Upper Two Medicine Lake.

> *The only ranger-led hike offered that I recommend for families in the Two Medicine Valley is the boat trip and hike to Upper Two Medicine Lake and No Name Lake. The boat takes you across Two Medicine Lake, and then you will hike*

with a ranger to Twin Falls and up to Upper Two Medicine Lake. This is an easy, mostly level, 4.4-mile hike with a 350-foot elevation gain. (Elevation gain is found in the National Park Service's Ranger-Led Activity Schedule.) Splurging for a boat ride will cut significant time off of the hike, and kids 3 and under are free. Call (406) 257-2426 for boat reservations. This is also a great hike to do without a ranger, on your own.

There is also the 2-mile round trip guided hike to Twin Falls available through the Glacier Park Boat Company.

Talks and Evening Programs in the Two Medicine Valley

The Two Medicine Campground has an amphitheater in Loop B, Site 40, that offers both ranger talks, and some evenings, members of the Blackfeet Tribe share their cultural histories and traditions with visitors via the Native America Speaks program. Check bulletin boards in the campground for specific topics. All talks last about 45 minutes. We love the Native America Speaks talks offered here.

Children's Programs in the Two Medicine Valley

The children's programs take place at the Two Medicine Amphitheater in Loop B, Site 40 in the Two Medicine Campground. These are recommended for children ages 5-12. These are short, only lasting for 20 – 30 minutes, and an adult needs to attend with the kids. These are a great way to get your children involved and for them to learn more about the Native Americans and protecting national parks. Check the Ranger-Led Activity Schedule for the month for the specific times and programs.

Camping in Two Medicine

The only campground available in the Two Medicine Valley is the Two Medicine Campground. Cut Bank Campground is 16 miles from East Glacier, over a winding pass so it does take some time to get between the campgrounds. If the Two Medicine Campground is full, you can use the Cut Bank Campground as a backup, and there are campgrounds available outside of the park in the town of East Glacier.

Two Medicine Campground

The Two Medicine Campground is found in the Two Medicine Valley 13 miles from East Glacier on Pray Lake, which is a small lake that runs off of Two Medicine Lake. This campground is one of the prettiest in the entire park. The campground is on a first-come, first-serve basis, and many campsites are right on the water.

Two Medicine Campground

This campground has 100 sites available. Potable water is available throughout the campground, and bathrooms have flush toilets and running water. Sites 1-36 are generator-free. There is a disposal station, but there are no showers. The summer camping season runs from early June to late September, and the primitive season runs until late October. During primitive season there is no potable water available.

47

The North Shore Trailhead leaves from the Two Medicine Campground, so you can hike right from the campground. Look up on the nearby mountain for black bears.

Pray Lake and Sinopah Mountain

There are nightly ranger-led programs at the amphitheater in the campground, and you can rent small boats from the Glacier Park Boat Co. located on Two Medicine Lake, a five-minute walk from the campground.

The Two Medicine Campground has become popular and fills usually by the middle of the day. Arrive early to be guaranteed a spot. If you arrive early and the campground signs say that the campground is full, keep in mind that this is not always updated early in the day, and be sure to drive through and check for available spots. Spots will become available as campers leave throughout the morning. Follow the lake to your left and head to the back of the campground to check availability for the campsites located on the water.

Glacier's Cut Bank Valley

Cut Bank Campground (tent only)

Cut Bank Campground is about 16 miles from East Glacier, between East Glacier and St. Mary. Unless you plan on doing some hiking in this area, none of which I recommend for families due to the remote location, and length of the trails, I would only stay at this campground if you needed a place to stay for the night.

You will travel north from East Glacier or south from St. Mary and will turn west at the Cut Bank sign, which will take you 5 miles along a gravel road. The drive up this valley is beautiful, with open meadows surrounded by forest and mountains. If you are looking to escape the crowds, the Cut Bank campground is the place to go.

Cut Bank Campground has only 14 sites available, all located in the trees. The campground is open from early June to late September. The campground is on a first-come, first-serve basis. It is considered to be in primitive camping status all summer because there is no potable water, so be sure to bring your own water. There is a pit toilet available.

Hotels

There are no hotels available in the Two Medicine Valley. You will have to travel to East Glacier and the surrounding area to find lodging.

Glacier Park Lodge

Glacier Park Lodge is a stunning historic lodge that features 161 guest rooms and can house over 500 people in East Glacier. Constructed in 1912, the lodge is a magnificent choice. You can expect smaller rooms and a quaint feeling from this older lodge, but this is to be expected from all of the historic lodges associated with Glacier National Park.

Glacier Park Lodge

Glacier Park Lodge features a 9-hole golf course, a swimming pool, a gift shop, dining, and a Remedies Day Spa. Be sure to ask whether the swimming pool will be open when booking a reservation, as it is not open the entire season. Even if you do not stay here, be sure to stop by for photos and to see the gigantic lobby, and the beautiful gardens out front.

The Great Northern Dining Room is in the lobby of the Glacier Park Lodge. While the attire is casual, it is more expensive than other places in town, and there are no reservations. They serve breakfast, lunch, and dinner, with a kids menu, and plenty of huckleberry drinks to choose from.

There is coffee and cocktails available in the lobby of the Glacier Park Lodge.

A box lunch is available for pickup from the Glacier Park Lodge. These are a packed lunch for you to take on the go, including a bottle of water, sandwich, and chips. Call (406) 892-2525 or order at the Lodge by 8 p.m. the day before pick-up.

Other Hotels in East Glacier

There are several hotel options in the town of East Glacier. Choices range from Dancing Bears Inn, the East Glacier Motel and Cabins, and the Mountain Pine Motel.

None of the lodging here is fancy, and all of the hotels will cost you around $200/night, just like all hotels anywhere in and around Glacier in the summer months. Choose one to use as a home base while you visit the Two Medicine Valley, or head up to the Two Medicine Campground and enjoy some nights in some of the best scenery in the state.

Upper Grinnell Lake and a portion of the Garden Wall

Chapter Six: Many Glacier

To come to Glacier National Park and miss Many Glacier would be a tragedy. Although Many Glacier is not on Going-to-the-Sun Road, the beauty and hiking opportunities here abound. While it may seem to be off the beaten path, the area buzzes with visitors all summer long, and I advise you to book hotels early and be aware that camping spots are nearly impossible to get.

The Many Glacier Entrance provides access to the Many Glacier Valley, the Many Glacier Hotel and restaurant, the Swiftcurrent Motor Inn, and the Many Glacier Campground. There are boat tours, horseback rides, and many ranger-led programs and talks available in this area. There is no visitor center in this part of the park.

Many Glacier embodies all that Glacier National Park has to offer. Here, you can hike to scenic waterfalls, lakes filled with icebergs in the summer, turquoise lakes, and the infamous Grinnell Glacier. You can ride horses, boats, see moose, grizzly bears, and stay in a historic lodge.

Many Glacier is tucked away in the northeastern corner of the park. If you do not have a vehicle, you can take the free shuttle to the St. Mary Visitor Center, and from there you can take the shuttle for a fee to Many Glacier. If you are driving, you will head north of St. Mary until you enter the tiny town of Babb, Montana. There is a small sign pointing you to Many Glacier just as you enter Babb. Turn west (left) and follow this road through the Many Glacier Entrance and on to Swiftcurrent Lake.

Keep in mind that you will NOT have cell phone service anywhere in the Many Glacier valley, including the hotels. There are payphones available. There is cell service available in the nearby towns of Babb and St. Mary.

View from the Grinnell Glacier Trail

Hiking

The Many Glacier area, home to Grinnell Glacier, Iceberg Lake, and the Ptarmigan Tunnel, is one of the most popular hiking areas in the Park. Most of the hikes in this area provide beautiful panoramic views, waterfalls, open meadows packed with wildflowers,

51

and the opportunity to see glaciers up close. The likelihood of seeing bears also makes Many Glacier a popular place. If you get the chance to visit Many Glacier, be sure to fit a hike into your trip. The following list includes family-friendly hikes as well as some that are longer and more difficult than I may usually recommend for those out of shape or traveling with young children, but they are worth the added effort!

Swiftcurrent Nature Trail

If you are looking for an easy, flat stroll, with gorgeous mountain views, the Swiftcurrent Nature Trail is for you! You can begin at the south end of the Many Glacier Hotel or at the Grinnell Glacier Trailhead about a half of a mile past the turn to the Many Glacier Hotel. The trail will loop around back to the Many Glacier Hotel.

This 3-mile round-trip trail will take you past several small beaches along Swiftcurrent Lake, and provide views of the mountains that Many Glacier is known for. Pack a lunch and enjoy your walk! Added bonus – our favorite beach in the park is just over the hill to Lake Josephine.

Grinnell Lake

If you take advantage of the available boat tours, this is a short, mostly flat hike to a cool turquoise lake. Its unique color is thanks to the glacial silt from the Grinnell Glacier above. Waterfalls cascade over the cliffs above and pour into the lake. From here you can see the Salamander Glacier and relax on the nice beach area at the outlet of the lake. The hike is about 1 mile each way if you take the boat tour to cut off some time. I highly recommend this hike for families with children. This is one of the most beautiful lakes in Glacier Park in my opinion!

The trailhead begins at the south end of the Many Glacier Hotel along Swiftcurrent Lake. However, I recommend taking the two boat tours offered by the Glacier Park Boat Company that cross Swiftcurrent Lake and Lake Josephine, cutting about 5 miles off of the hike to Grinnell Lake. There is a fee to take the boats, but it is well worth the money to save the time and miles! The boat tours are fun and informative. Remember that the boat only runs for a few months during the summer. If you visit when the boat is not running or choose to bypass the boat, this is a manageable fairly

Grinnell Lake

Swiftcurrent Lake and Grinnell Point

level 7-mile hike round-trip leaving from Grinnell Glacier Trailhead.

The Glacier Park Boat Company will drop you off at the head of Lake Josephine. Depart the boat and follow the trail to your right and follow the signs to Grinnell Lake. The hike will take you mostly through the forest, but you will get to cross over beautiful creeks, including one with a swinging bridge that kids will enjoy.

There is a short detour to Hidden Falls near the swinging bridge. The trail says 0.3-miles each way, but it is just a short walk up the hill to see a beautiful waterfall tucked into a tight ravine. We saw steaming bear scat on this short side trail to Hidden Falls the last time we hiked it. The creek at the base of the falls is where you will find the swinging bridge, and the water is so clear and beautiful here.

There is also the option of taking the guided hike to Grinnell Lake provided with the boat tour by the Glacier Park Boat Company.

Note that the Grinnell Lake Trail and the Grinnell Glacier Trail are separate trails. You won't pass directly by Grinnell Lake on your way to the Grinnell Glacier. However, you will see Grinnell Lake from above if you hike to the Grinnell Glacier.

One year on our hike to Grinnell Lake we almost got run over by a cow moose and her calf on the trail. About 10 minutes after we got off the boat, we heard an odd pounding on the trail behind us, what sounded like a person running up the trail. The forest and undergrowth was thick where we stopped, so by the time we knew what the noise was, a cow moose and her calf were barreling down on us less than 15 yards away. Thankfully, the mother veered off the trail at the last second, leaping into the creek before she steamrolled us. We then were fortunate to watch her and her calf eat, drink, and meander downstream for several minutes.

If you are looking for an easy, pretty hike and want to see a beautiful lake, especially if traveling with small children, I highly recommend the hike to Grinnell Lake!

Grinnell Glacier

Grinnell Glacier is one of the most popular hikes in Glacier, as the trail leads directly to one of the Park's disappearing glaciers. This hike provides outstanding views and the opportunity to walk right up to the Grinnell Glacier, and affords close-up views of the Salamander Glacier, and the smaller Gem Glacier.

This is at the top of my list for must-see hikes in Glacier National Park for families. Not only do you get to see a glacier, you also get the incredible scenery that Upper Grinnell Lake provides from the melting glacier.

The hike to Grinnell Glacier is 7.6 miles round-trip - if you take the boat tour across Swiftcurrent Lake and Lake Josephine for a fee – or approximately 11 miles round-trip if you hike from the trailhead and do not take the boat. This hike has an elevation gain of 1,840 feet, according to hikinginglacier.com. Other websites have the elevation gain listed as 2,400 feet, so be aware that this may be significant elevation gain for some visitors.

Hiking to Grinnell Glacier

The trailhead for Grinnell Glacier is about a half of a mile past the turn to the Many Glacier Hotel. Parking can be difficult to find here, so start your hike early in the day. If you begin at the trailhead, you will hike around Swiftcurrent Lake and then around Lake Josephine before you follow the trail up to Grinnell Glacier. The hike around these lakes is flat and beautiful, and if you are up for the distance, I recommend doing the entire hike and skipping the boat.

> If traveling with small children, I highly recommend taking the boat trip with the Glacier Park Boat Company to shave significant distance off of your trip. This means that you should try to catch the earliest boat tour, leaving from the Many Glacier Hotel at 8:30 a.m. Park behind the hotel and be sure to arrive 15 minutes early to board the boat. The boat trip will take you across Swiftcurrent Lake, and then you will have a short hike over to Lake Josephine, where you will board the "Morning Eagle" boat. Depart the boat at the head of Lake Josephine, and begin your hike from there. (There is a fee for these boat trips, but children under 4 are free.)

Follow the Grinnell Glacier Trail signs on the trail as you depart the boat. This hike has views of Grinnell Lake, Grinnell Falls, Lake Josephine, and Lake Sherburne far down the valley. There are a few spots where the trail is narrow, but this trail is safe and should not scare anyone who isn't too afraid of heights. You will reach a spot near the end of the hike where there is a pit toilet and some benches, but this is not the end. Continue hiking until you reach Upper Grinnell Lake, and the Grinnell Glacier.

This may be a big hike for smaller kids, due to the length and elevation gain. The trail is exposed the entire way, meaning that you will be in the sun with little shade, making it a hot hike in the middle of summer. If you start early to avoid the heat, and pack plenty of water, most families should be able to do this hike. Grinnell Glacier is a fantastic hike, one of the best in the park.

If you are concerned about the sketchier parts of this hike, another option is to hike around two miles from Lake Josephine up the trail toward Grinnell Glacier to a spot where there is an overlook looking down at Grinnell Lake below.

The Glacier Park Boat Company also provides a guided hike to Grinnell Glacier.

Arriving at Iceberg Lake

Iceberg Lake

Iceberg Lake is also one of the most popular trails in Glacier. Iceberg Lake is a 10-mile round-trip hike with an elevation gain of 1,200 feet. Here you can count on panoramic mountain views, waterfalls, wildflowers, and the well-known Iceberg Lake, boasting a stunning blue color full of ice nearly year-round. The lake is tucked deep in a cirque, and due to the surrounding mountains above, the lake receives little sunshine, allowing floating "icebergs" to remain throughout most of the summer.

The trailhead to Iceberg Lake begins behind the Swiftcurrent Motor Inn. There is a road leading you behind the inn, with about 15 parking spots available. If this is full, then you will park out in front of the Swiftcurrent Motor Inn in the main parking lot. The earlier you start hiking in the day, the better the parking opportunities. This parking lot is always full in the middle of the day during the busy season.

This hike provides incredible views of the Swiftcurrent Valley as you go. Most of the elevation is gained in the beginning of the hike, but then it is a gradual, pleasant incline for the remaining several miles. So don't let the first section deter you!

Small waterfalls trickle over the trail along the way, and you will have the opportunity to pick huckleberries right off the trail as you go.

There are beautiful flowers at Iceberg Lake

Approximately halfway you will reach Ptarmigan Falls, a pretty waterfall that you can just barely see the top of from the trail as you approach. The view from the trail is the best view you will have, as the trail takes you to the creek just above the falls. This spot along the creek is a perfect place to stop for lunch or a snack before you continue on to the lake.

The icebergs will melt in the lake by the end of the summer. Some years, the ice melts even earlier. We hiked this in the middle of July 2015, and the ice was already melted thanks to the warm year. It is still a gorgeous hike, with beautiful views the entire way and the lake is a beautiful color and worth the hike even if the ice has melted by the time you get there.

> *Tip: It is cold at Iceberg Lake! While you are hiking it will be hot, and then as you approach the lake, the temperature drops significantly. I would recommend bringing a warm jacket, especially for children, so you can picnic and explore around the lake without freezing. Also be sure to pack hats and sunglasses, as this hike is exposed to the sun for most of the way. There is a nice beach area as you approach Iceberg Lake that tends to get crowded because everyone stops here. There is a side trail to your left that will take you partially around the lake to a less crowded spot.*

Do not walk on the icebergs. In years where a lot of icebergs remained, we have seen people jump from iceberg to iceberg to get to the middle of the lake. If you were to fall off of an iceberg, you would probably not be able to climb back up onto the iceberg and you would not survive in the cold water. Just take my word for it and stay off of the icebergs.

Apikuni Falls

Apikuni Falls is a short but fairly steep hike to a tall waterfall that plunges 100 feet over a cliff into a couple of tiers. The hike is under two-miles round-trip, and quickly gains about 700 feet in elevation. Depending on what kind of shape you are in, this hike may make your legs burn, as you gain a lot of elevation in a short distance. But the fact that it is short makes it manageable for anyone.

The hike to Apikuni Falls begins just before you reach the turn to the Many Glacier Hotel after entering the park via the Many Glacier Entrance at the Poia Lake trailhead. There is

Apikuni Falls

limited parking available in the pull-out at this spot, but it doesn't seem to be full too often.

I love this hike because while you will travel through a lot of trees, you will also be provided beautiful views of the mountains towering over the Many Glacier Hotel behind you. You are able to climb over some rocks to get close to the waterfall.

The last time we hiked to Apikuni Falls we got caught in a hailstorm near the waterfall and had to find cover. This was also the time we forgot the Ergobaby baby carrier, so I had to carry our one-month-old baby in a sling I made out of a blanket. Always be prepared for the weather and bring layers, just in case!

Cracker Lake

If you are up for doing a longer hike in the Many Glacier area, Cracker Lake is an excellent choice. This hike will take you up about 1400 feet in elevation, for a total of 12 and half miles round-trip. The hike itself is mostly through the trees, so you won't encounter as many dynamic views while hiking as some of the other hikes in Many Glacier. But at the end of the trail you begin to break through the timberline and are greeted with the stunning green waters of Cracker Lake, nestled beneath the 10,000-foot Mt. Siyeh and 9,300-foot Allen Mountain.

This is one of the longer hikes recommended in this book insofar as pointing you to "family friendly" activities in Glacier. Deciding to tackle this hike will depend on hiking ability and ages of your children. Swan Mountain Outfitters offers a day-trip horseback ride to the lake. This will take an entire day, but is easier than hiking yourself, and you still get to see this gorgeous lake while trying your hand at horseback riding.

Cracker Lake

If you do hike it, keep in mind that the start of the trail can be quite muddy from the horses, so you may prefer waterproof boots or shoes for this hike.

The trailhead to Cracker Lake is at the south end of the Many Glacier Hotel parking lot.

Fishercap Lake

Fishercap Lake is one of the best places to see moose in Glacier. This small lake has views looking up into the Swiftcurrent Valley. You will park near the Swiftcurrent Motor Inn and take the trail leading to Swiftcurrent Pass and Red Rock Falls. The trail to Fishercap Lake is flat and only takes about ten minutes each way. The best time to see moose, as with most wildlife, is early morning or in the evening. This is such an easy hike and there is a nice beach area. We stop here often for a picnic lunch, and usually try to take a walk here in the evenings to look for moose.

Fishercap Lake

Red Rock Falls

Hiking to Red Rock Falls is one of my most highly recommended hikes for families in Glacier National Park. The trail is mostly flat, and is about 2 miles each way. Red Rock Falls is not a tall waterfall, but it has several cascading tiers and there are trails going right up to the falls. Kids will enjoy the opportunity to stick their feet in the water and there are great photo opportunities.

Red Rock Falls

This hike takes you past Fishercap Lake, and the beautiful Red Rock Lake. A lot of the hike is in the trees, but there are several views up the Swiftcurrent Valley. It is a pretty and pleasant hike for everyone, and both lakes have nice beaches to picnic and let the kids wade and play.

The trailhead is located at the far end of the parking lot past the Swiftcurrent Motor Inn, at the end of Many Glacier Road. Parking here is usually full in the middle of the day. Go early in the morning or the evening for better parking opportunities.

Bullhead Lake

Bullhead Lake is another beautiful lake that is past Fishercap Lake and Red Rock Falls. Glacier National Park's signs for this hike show that the length is 7.8 miles round-trip. Other websites list it as just over 7 miles round-trip. Either way, with a minimal elevation gain of 500 feet, you won't notice the length.

The hike is fairly easy, and has beautiful mountain views the entire

Bullhead Lake

way. You will pass Fishercap Lake and Red Rock Lake, that offer nice beaches for kids to wade. Then you will pass Red Rock Falls. If you plan on hiking to Red Rock Falls, but also want a longer hike, this is an option. Waterfalls will cascade from the mountains surrounding you as you go. There is not great kid-friendly beach access for small children at Bullhead Lake, so if you are looking for a shorter hike to dip your feet in, you should stop at Red Rock Falls and not continue all of the way to Bullhead Lake.

The Bullhead Lake trailhead begins at the end of the Swiftcurrent Motor Inn parking lot, and is the same trail that takes you to Swiftcurrent Pass.

Programs and Activities

There are several programs offered in this area for families to enjoy. Read more about what the Glacier National Park programs entail in Chapter Two. Glacier often changes its programs, so the list of programs here may change at any time. Be sure to check the current Ranger-Led Activity Schedule for the month you are visiting to check the available dates and times of each program listed here.

Boat Rentals

Boats are available for rent at Many Glacier from the Glacier Boat Company; including canoes, single or double kayaks, and rowboats. Rent a boat and explore Swiftcurrent Lake, looking back at views of the Many Glacier Hotel. If you bring your own boat, I have seen people take it up the shallow creek from Swiftcurrent Lake to Lake Josephine. The Glacier Boat Company does not allow their boats to travel up the creek. Another option for getting your own boat to Lake Josephine is to carry it over the trail between the two lakes.

Boat Tour (and Boat Tours with Guided Hikes)

I highly recommend taking the 1 ½ hour boat tour offered in Many Glacier. The Glacier Park Boat Company offers a Many Glacier tour that includes two tours: "Chief Two Guns" that tours Swiftcurrent Lake, and the "Morning Eagle" that crosses Lake Josephine.

The "Morning Eagle" is the last boat that will run on Lake Josephine; once this boat breaks down, there will no longer be boat tours on this lake. You won't see Lake Josephine without a boat tour unless you are willing to hike around Swiftcurrent Lake, and Lake Josephine is stunning.

There are many options for boating at Many Glacier

The boat tour provides funny commentary, interesting information about the boat company, the wooden boats, and the surrounding glaciers and mountains. Not only do these boats provide fun tours of these lakes, but they also provide access to many trails, including the Grinnell Glacier and Grinnell Lake hikes.

Many Glacier boat tours are popular and fill quickly. Glacier Park Boat Company requires you to make reservations three days in advance at this location to guarantee a seat. Call the Glacier Park Boat Company at (406) 257-2426 to make a reservation. If tickets are still available, you can book upon arrival at the boat dock located just below the Many Glacier Hotel on Swiftcurrent Lake. They do start waitlists to fill the boats with empty seats at the last minute.

Kids love the boat tours

There are several tour times offered throughout the summer, and some of the tours include optional guided hikes to Grinnell Glacier or Grinnell Lake. The boat tour is more expensive at Many Glacier than other tours in the park, because you get two boat tours at this location. Children ages 0-3 are free.

> TIP: Sometimes parking can be difficult to find at the Many Glacier Hotel to take a boat tour. Allow 20 extra minutes in case you have to park a distance away so that you don't miss the boat.

Note that there is a distance between the two lakes where you depart one boat and walk to catch the next boat on Lake Josephine. This requires walking up a short hill of 0.2 miles.

If you are not getting off the boat to hike, you will remain on the boat at the end of Lake Josephine and return back to the Many Glacier Hotel. If you are planning on hiking: once you get to the head of Lake Josephine, you will unload from the boat. **BE SURE if you are hiking to get the colored return ticket. This ticket is your return ticket to get on the boats on the way back.** The blue ticket will give you the return times that the boat will be sure to have room for hikers.

If you miss the return boat, you can hike either trail around Lake Josephine by following the signs to get back to the Many Glacier Hotel. The faster way to get back to the hotel is by taking the right shoreline when you are facing Lake Josephine.

> FOR THE KIDS: Grab your kid a "Passport" and a free postcard from the hut where you bought your tickets on your way off the boat at Many Glacier Hotel.

Ranger-Led Walks and Hikes

The Many Glacier area has several hikes and walks that offer gorgeous lakes, waterfalls, and glaciers. Read more about what the Glacier National Park programs entail in Chapter Two. Be sure to check the current Ranger-Led Activity Schedule to check the current programs and the available dates and times.

Here are some examples of ranger-led activities that Glacier National Park has had in prior years in Many Glacier.

Early Morning Bird Walk

The Early Morning Bird Walk is a fun walk if you are interested in birds. A ranger will walk with you and help you identify the local birds. It is recommended you bring binoculars and a field guide. You will meet at the boat dock behind the Many Glacier Hotel. Plan on 3 hours for this walk, with a round-trip length of 3 miles. This walk is not available very often, so be sure to check a ranger-led activity schedule to find out when it is available.

Heart of Glacier Hike (Hike to Iceberg Lake)

The Heart of Glacier Hike is a popular hike that will lead you to the stunning Iceberg Lake. Iceberg Lake is one of the most popular trails in Glacier National Park, and if you want to do it with a ranger, this is your chance! Rangers are great because they provide a lot of information, but keep in mind that you will be in a line of people hiking and have to keep pace with them, whether fast or slow. Plan on 7 hours for this 10-mile hike.

Hiking on the Iceberg / Ptarmigan Trail

Nature Walk

The Nature Walk is a great walk to take with kids. A ranger will take you on a 1-hour, easy 1-mile walk to Wilbur Falls and Fishercap Lake.

Wildflower Walk

Learn all about the area's wildflowers on this 2-hour, 2-mile walk near Swiftcurrent Lake. Meet at the Grinnell Glacier trailhead in the Many Glacier picnic area.

Boat Tours with Guided Hikes

The Glacier Park Boat Company offers guided hikes to both Grinnell Lake and Grinnell Glacier.

Talks and Evening Programs

Be sure to check the current ranger-led activity schedule for dates and times in the month you are visiting the park.

Where Have All the Glaciers Gone?

Glaciers and their retreat in the park are a main topic of interest for visitors. To learn more about the glaciers over the years, you will meet a ranger in the Many Glacier Hotel lobby for an hour.

Sherburne Reservoir and peaks of Many Glacier

Photo courtesy of Blake Passmore

Jack Gladstone's "Triple Divide: Heritage and Legacy"

Jack Gladstone is a Blackfeet Tribal member who puts on an entertaining show of song and stories exploring tribal history and animal legends. His one-hour show usually takes place in the Many Glacier Hotel Lucerne Room.

Native America Speaks

Anyone is welcome to the free "Native America Speaks" program at the Many Glacier Campground Amphitheater. On certain nights, usually one night a week, this program takes the place of the evening ranger talk, and you will have the opportunity to hear from members of the Blackfeet Tribe as they share their history and traditions. These programs last 45 minutes. We love these programs; I find them particularly fascinating.

Many Glacier Hotel Evening Talk

In the Many Glacier Hotel Lucerne Room, visitors gather to learn about various topics covered by park rangers at no cost. These 45-minute programs are similar to the campground ranger talks, but this is fun to attend if you are staying at the Many Glacier Hotel or if there is inclement weather and you prefer to attend an indoor talk. You can check bulletin boards for the specific topic. This program is offered several nights of the week, but be sure to check the ranger-led activity schedule for updated information. Everyone is welcome.

Many Glacier Campground Ranger Talk

Like many campgrounds in Glacier, the Many Glacier Campground offers a ranger talk in the evenings to learn more about the natural and cultural history of the park. This will take place in the Many Glacier Campground Amphitheater for about 45 minutes. To find out what topics will be discussed during your visit, check the bulletin board located in the campground. Non-campers are always welcome.

Spotting Scope Programs

There is often a ranger available during the evening hours on certain nights of the summer where visitors can stop by the Swiftcurrent Motor Inn parking lot and use the spotting scopes to look for animals and ask a ranger about the animals in Glacier. This is a great way to see bears and mountain goats, especially if you didn't bring your own binoculars.

Children's Programs

Children's programs are not always offered at Many Glacier, so be sure to check the Ranger-Led Activity Schedule for the month you are visiting to see if they are being offered. Children's Programs are great for families and children, but an adult must attend with children. These are recommended for kids between the ages of 5 and 12, and usually take place in the Many Glacier Campground Amphitheater.

Hotel Tour

Many Glacier offers a unique program that tours the Many Glacier Hotel to learn about its history and restoration. Many Glacier celebrated its 100th anniversary in 2015, and we happened to be there – on the Fourth of July! This is a free one-hour program that will require walking some stairs around the hotel. The Many Glacier Hotel has incredible history, and this walk is great for some laughs and history. For this program, you will meet in the Many Glacier Hotel lobby.

Camping at Many Glacier Campground

Camping

The only camping available in the Many Glacier valley is the Many Glacier campground. There are several options for camping just outside of Many Glacier around Babb and St. Mary if you are unable to find a camping spot upon arrival at Many Glacier. The St. Mary KOA is a popular choice that allows reservations.

While most of the campsites in Many Glacier are available on a first-come, first-serve basis, in 2016 Glacier National Park began allowing visitors to book 41 campsites in advance The campsites can be booked up to six months in advance on **recreation.gov/**. Be sure to look carefully at the facility map and site list to ensure the specific campsite you book will accommodate your vehicle. Only a limited number of campsites can accommodate larger vehicles and towed units. Note also that some of the sites do not allow generator use. The remaining 62 campsites will be available first-come, first-serve as you arrive.

The Many Glacier Campground is arguably the most popular campground in Glacier. There are only 109 campsites available, and most of the campground is on a first-come, first-serve basis. This campground will fill as early as 7 a.m., so it is highly recommended that you arrive early if you want to camp at this location. I have been involved in the stress of trying to find a campsite here, and competing with others to get a spot is not enjoyable while on vacation.

The campground is in the trees, so you will have plenty of shade and each site has the usual picnic table and fire ring. The best part about this campground is its location; walk out of your tent and you can begin hiking to some of the most popular day hikes in Glacier, including Grinnell Glacier and Iceberg Lake. It is also convenient for evening strolls to check for moose at Fishercap Lake.

This campground is also not far from the historic Many Glacier Hotel, which has a nice restaurant, boat tours, horseback riding, and Red Bus tours. There is a casual Italian restaurant with a gift shop and a camp store filled with basic food at the Swiftcurrent Motor Inn just across the road from the campground. The free shuttle service does not connect to Many Glacier, but you can catch a shuttle for a fee to connect you with other east side destinations.

The Many Glacier Campground is open from late May to late September. Primitive camping is available from the end of the summer season to the end of October. During primitive camping, there is no drinking water available and the fee is less expensive than during the summer season.

Some of the campsites here are generator-free. The campground has a disposal station and sinks with running water and flush toilets, but no showers. There are showers available for a fee near the Swiftcurrent Motor Inn.

The Many Glacier Campground has a nightly ranger-led talk for free; check the bulletin boards in the campground for the nightly topic. You can find more information on the ranger-led activities in the ranger-guided activity schedule provided to you at the entrances or visitor centers in Glacier National Park. Many Glacier is the best place to see bears in Glacier, so I recommend bringing binoculars, and bear spray.

Camping at Many Glacier

Many Glacier Hotel and Wynn Mountain

Hotels

Many Glacier Hotel

Many Glacier Hotel sits along the shores of Swiftcurrent Lake in the Many Glacier Valley. This hotel is a National Historic Landmark and is similar to a Swiss chalet with the stunning mountains as a backdrop and its decor.

The rooms themselves at this hotel are best described as rustic. You will notice on many websites, including TripAdvisor, that people are often disappointed with the size and quality of the rooms. This hotel is quite expensive, but this is the price you pay to walk out your door and be on the shores of one of the most beautiful scenes in all of Glacier National Park. You can count on the rooms being small. Splurge on a lakeside room with a shared balcony to enjoy the views any time of the day.

Many Glacier Hotel has a restaurant, offering lakeside tables with views of the surrounding mountains. The Many Glacier Hotel restaurant does not accept reservations, so you may be put on a waitlist if you want dinner around 7pm or later. There is also a bar available for cocktails. Personally, I like to grab a cocktail and enjoy it out on the porch overlooking Swiftcurrent Lake. The Many Glacier Hotel restaurant is pricier than most in Glacier National Park, so if you have small children or are on a budget, I recommend going up to the Swiftcurrent Motor Inn Italian Garden for dinner.

Many Glacier Hotel also has a small shop in the basement that offers quick snacks similar to a convenience store.

> *INSIDER'S TIP FOR LAST MINUTE ROOMS:*
>
> *The Many Glacier Hotel books months in advance. It is nearly impossible to get a hotel room last minute online or by calling. However, if you are in the area and are hoping for a room for the night, be sure to stop by the hotel and ask at the front desk. They reserve a few rooms in the basement for drop-ins so they don't have to turn everyone away. They may not be fancy rooms, but at least you will have a place to stay for the night!*

Swiftcurrent Motor Inn and Cabins

Swiftcurrent Motor Inn and Cabins is found in the trees just one mile from Many Glacier Hotel. This is an affordable option for a family looking to stay in the Many Glacier area without having to camp. There are 88 motel-style rooms and small cottages offered with or without bathrooms.

Here you will also find an Italian-style restaurant serving pizza and pasta, as well as a gift shop and a store to buy limited amenities. There is also a public shower for a fee (if you don't stay at the Inn) and laundry facilities available.

The Swiftcurrent Motor Inn is located right at the trailhead to 11 trails, including the popular Iceberg Lake Trail. The proximity to these trails makes this a great place to stay for those planning on hiking. Walk out the door and start hiking. There are also family friendly hikes leaving from here, like the hike to Red Rock Falls. The parking lot in front of the Inn is what you will use to get to several hiking trails, even if you are not staying at the Swiftcurrent Motor Inn.

Swiftcurrent Motor Inn

Wading in Red Rock Lake

Animals in Many Glacier

The Many Glacier area is the best spot in the park to see grizzly bears and black bears. The hillsides above the Many Glacier Hotel and the Iceberg Lake Trail usually have bears that you can view well using binoculars. The road from the Many Glacier Entrance to Many Glacier Hotel is also a great place for spotting bears. I have seen countless bears crossing the road to get down to Lake Sherburne.

Fishercap Lake is one of the best places in Glacier to see moose. All of the lakes in this area are ripe with moose, but Fishercap has a predictable moose family that frequents the lake at first light and in the early evening. Be sure to take the ten-minute walk down to see the moose during your visit.

Chief Mountain Highway: Many Glacier to Waterton

This book does not cover Waterton Lakes National Park. However, if you do plan on visiting the stunning Waterton Lakes Park, you will use the Chief Mountain Highway that starts 13 miles north of St. Mary. You will turn off of US-89 at the sign onto Chief Mountain Highway just past Babb, Montana. This 26-mile road is a beautiful scenic drive that provides views of Chief Mountain. The Chief Mountain Highway will take you about an hour to get into Waterton, depending on how long the border crossing into Canada takes.

Keep in mind that Waterton Lakes National Park is a separate park that is in Canada, so you will need your passport to cross the border, and it has a separate entrance fee from Glacier National Park.

A day trip is manageable if you are staying on the east side of Glacier National Park. Chief Mountain Highway is open from the middle of May to the end of September.

Grizzly bear in Many Glacier

Sunrift Gorge
Photo courtesy of Blake Passmore

Chapter Seven:
St. Mary

Similar to other towns bordering Glacier National Park, St. Mary is a small town located on the east side near the St. Mary Entrance to the Park. The St. Mary Entrance is the east entry point to Going-to-the-Sun Road, providing access to the St. Mary Visitor Center, St. Mary Lake, and the St. Mary and Rising Sun Campgrounds. The St. Mary Entrance is what I consider to be the East Entrance. This small town offers beautiful views into the mountains of Glacier, and is dotted with a few hotels, a few restaurants and gift shops, and two fuel stations.

Hiking

While there are several hikes between St. Mary and Logan Pass, there are three hikes that I recommend most for families. They all include a waterfall, and are manageable for those with kids or anyone looking for a fairly easy hike. The trailheads are all conveniently located along Going-to-the-Sun Road not far from Logan Pass.

Note that the Reynolds Creek Fire of 2015 may have a significant impact on the hikes and features listed here.

St. Mary Falls/Virginia Falls

I list St. Mary Falls and Virginia Falls together because they are along the same trail, and you have to hike past St. Mary Falls to get to Virginia Falls. Just over three miles roundtrip will get you all of the way to Virginia Falls and back to the trailhead.

Both of these hikes begin at the St. Mary Falls trailhead along Going-to-the-Sun Road, nearly 11 miles from the St. Mary Entrance. Since parking at this trailhead is limited, and these waterfalls are extremely popular, especially in the middle of the day, I recommend either arriving early or catching the free shuttle offered by the Park Service that will drop you off at the trailhead.

Glacier is now encouraging use of the free shuttle and has actually made the parking area that was at the St. Mary Falls trailhead a shuttle stop only. The next parking area to the east, the Gunsight Lake trailhead, will be where you want to park. You can begin hiking from here and follow the signs to get to St. Mary Falls. Just watch when you are hiking back, the first sign that points to Going-to-the-Sun Road on your way back will take you up to the shuttle stop. If you parked in the Gunsight Lake lot and you use that trail, you will end up having to walk a short distance along Going-to-the-Sun Road to get back to your vehicle. The pavement is hot and there is too much traffic. You will want to keep hiking on the main trail to the next fork and take the left at that fork to get back up to your vehicle if you don't want to end up walking along Going-to-the-Sun Road.

The trail begins by hiking through a small meadow with beautiful views of the surrounding peaks, including Dusty Star Mountain and Little Chief Mountain. The hike heads down into the forest, where you will remain until you reach the St. Mary River and then the St. Mary Falls. Here you can cross the footbridge and get fairly close to the base of St. Mary Falls.

St. Mary Falls drops in a couple of tiers, and there are great opportunities for photos. It gets crowded later in the day, so arrive early for the best photo opportunities.

Don't stop there! Keep going to Virginia Falls, a massive waterfall that you can get close enough to feel the spray. To get to Virginia Falls, just continue following the trail past St. Mary Falls, where it heads slightly uphill past several small unnamed waterfalls until you eventually reach Virginia Falls.

Virginia Falls drops roughly 50-feet, and is quite incredible because you can hike right up to it. Early in the season when flow is heavy, the force and spray from the falls is significant. You can also cross the creek using the bridge just below the falls and have a nice view with a beach to eat lunch where you are farther from the spray of the waterfall.

Virginia Falls

Baring Falls

Baring Falls is a pretty waterfall that is just a short walk from the parking area on Going-to-the-Sun Road. Park at the Sunrift Gorge, and follow the Siyeh Pass trail down 0.4 miles each way.

St. Mary Falls

You will take a right at the only junction on the trail, cross over the footbridge that leads over Baring Creek, and then you will see the 25-foot waterfall. This is a nice place for a picnic. Those looking for more should follow the trail a short distance farther down to St. Mary Lake for gorgeous views of the surrounding mountains and beach.

Finding a parking spot here can be difficult. There is limited parking along Going-to-the-Sun Road, and it is always full in the middle of the day. Get an early start to ensure you will have a place to park.

If you can't find parking, or want to hike to Baring Falls as part of a tour, remember that the Glacier Park Boat Company offers a hike to both Baring Falls and St. Mary Falls from their St. Mary Lake boat tours.

Baring Falls

The Piegan Pass Trail has spectacular scenery

Piegan Pass

Piegan Pass is an enjoyable family hike that is easily overlooked and provides incredible views of Glacier National Park. This hike is just over 9 miles round-trip if you hike from Siyeh Bend to the pass and back to your vehicle, with around a 1,850-foot elevation gain.

The trail begins at Siyeh Bend, which is just over two miles east side of Logan Pass, on Going-to-the-Sun Road. Parking is limited, so I would start early for this hike.

The hike begins for a short distance following Siyeh Creek, and then you will turn and begin to hike through the forest for several miles. This is where the majority of the elevation is gained. Follow the signs at a few forks in the trail to continue toward Piegan Pass.

After you pass the fork that splits to go toward either Siyeh Pass or Piegan Pass, you emerge from the trees and have amazing views the rest of your hike of Going-to-the-Sun Road, and a few glaciers that still exist at the time of this writing. From here the trail is mostly level all of the way to the pass.

You also have the option of hiking from Siyeh Bend over Piegan Pass and all of the way to the Many Glacier Hotel. This would add miles to your trip, but this hike is incredibly beautiful with the valley views on the other side as well as waterfalls.

When I hiked over Piegan Pass in September 2015, we encountered six grizzlies on or near the trail. If you plan on hiking this late in the season when there are fewer people, be sure to travel in groups and carry bear spray.

> *Important Tip: When you get to Piegan Pass, be sure to walk just beyond the pass along the trail over the other side. Here you will get a beautiful view of a tiny blue unnamed lake that has some of the most amazing color out of any of the lakes found in Glacier National Park!*

The other side of Piegan Pass

Programs

There are several programs offered in this area of Glacier National Park for families to enjoy. Read more about what the Glacier National Park programs entail in Chapter Two. Glacier National Park often changes their programs, so the list of programs here may change at any time. The following programs are examples of programs that Glacier National Park has had in the past. Be sure to check the current year's Ranger-Led Activity Schedule for the month you are visiting to check the available dates and times of the current programs.

RANGER-LED WALKS AND HIKES

A Walk on the Wild Side

Join a ranger for an easy one-mile hike from Sunrift Gorge to Sun Point, following along the shore of St. Mary Lake. This is a great way to find out information about this area, and is a hike that anyone can handle. Enjoy Baring Falls and the mountains surrounding St. Mary Lake. Set aside 2 hours for this 2-mile round-trip hike, making use of the free park shuttle if possible because parking is limited. Meet at the Sunrift Gorge parking area.

A Great Disturbance in the Forest Hike

If you are looking for a slightly longer hike, join a park ranger for the 3-mile Beaver Pond loop trail starting from the 1913 Ranger Station Parking lot. This easy walk will take about 2.5 hours, and will take you through meadows and woods to learn about wildflowers and wildlife, and the destructive forces that create balance in these forests.

Sunrise on St. Mary Lake and Wild Goose Island

Evening Programs

All evening programs last 45 minutes and are located in the Rising Sun Campground Amphitheater and St. Mary Campground Amphitheater nightly. These offer a chance to interact with a ranger and learn more about the history of the park. The following evening programs are free to all, and non-campers are always welcome. For non-campers, parking space is limited.

Native America Speaks

Members of the local Blackfeet Tribe share their history and traditions with visitors at the Rising Sun Campground Amphitheater. This is not a nightly event; this series only takes place on certain nights. On the other nights, a ranger-led talk will take place. You can check the Native America Speaks schedule online at **nps.gov/glac**, or by checking the Ranger-Led Activity Schedule for the month you are visiting.

Rising Sun Campground Ranger Talk

As with most campgrounds in Glacier, the Rising Sun Campground offers a free evening ranger talk at the Rising Sun Campground Amphitheater on various topics to learn about the history of the park. Check bulletin boards in the campground for specific topics each night.

St. Mary Campground Ranger Talk

St. Mary Campground also offers a nightly ranger talk at the St. Mary Campground amphitheater in Loop C. This is a fun way for kids and adults to learn about various topics of importance to Glacier National Park. Find the nightly topic on the bulletin board in the campground.

Sky Viewing Programs

The Sky Viewing Programs are located in the St. Mary Visitor Center parking lot, and one of the few opportunities for this type of program in Glacier. There has been a day program and a night program offered at no cost.

Half the Park Happens After Dark

The Half The Park Happens After Dark program is offered on clear nights later in the evening. There will be an astronomer present to talk about why it is important to protect our night skies and to talk about stars and what you see. Viewing will begin as soon as it gets dark and goes for a few hours. The Park Service requests you arrive before viewing time.

Here Comes the Sun

On sunny days a rangers may have a special solar telescope available for viewing the sun, and learning its importance to life on Earth. Meet at the St. Mary Visitor Center parking. Check the Ranger-Led Activity Schedule for the month you are visiting for specific dates.

The Milky Way
Photo courtesy of Blake Passmore

CHILDREN'S PROGRAMS

The Children's programs are designed specifically for families and those with children. An adult must attend with the children. These programs are set up for children between the ages of 5 and 12, and last for 20 to 30 minutes. These are great programs for getting kids involved and helping them learn more about the animals and history of Glacier National Park. Once your child completes their Junior Ranger booklet, be sure to stop by to get them sworn in as a Junior Ranger.

Boat Tours

There are no non-motorized boats available for rent on St. Mary Lake.

The Glacier Park Boat Company offers a 1.5-hour boat trip around St. Mary Lake. This trip will get you a view of the Sexton Glacier, a close-up view of the popular Wild Goose Island, and remnants of the Great Northern Railway President Louis Hill's private cabin. Not to mention the stunning mountains that surround St. Mary Lake.

This tour begins at the Rising Sun boat dock right off Going-to-the-Sun Road, five miles from the eastern entrance at the town of St. Mary. The St. Mary boat dock has plenty of parking right by the boat dock; accommodating RV's, tour buses, and camper trailers. You will find bathrooms behind the ticket office.

One-way tickets are available only for return boat trips, not for up-lake travel from the main dock. One-way tickets are sold on a space available basis. This would be a great option if you catch the free shuttle up to the trailheads, complete your hikes to St. Mary Falls and Virginia Falls, and then want to take the boat back.

Rising Sun Boat Launch, photo courtesy of Blake Passmore

As always, there is no food or beverages sold on the boat, so be sure to bring your own! There are also no bathrooms on the boat.

Boat tour with hike: Some of the tours offer an optional hike to Baring Falls. If this is offered on your trip, I recommend taking it, because the pretty waterfall is just a short walk from the lake! Some of the tours will offer an optional hiking trip to St. Mary Falls, which is 3 miles round-trip. These hikes are included with the cost of the boat tour if you choose to partake.

Tip: St. Mary Lake can be cold and windy. The wind seems to funnel down from Logan Pass. Bring a warm jacket for this boat ride, just in case!

Camping

There are two campgrounds inside of the park near St. Mary. The St. Mary Campground is closer to the town of St. Mary and the St. Mary Entrance. The Rising Sun Campground is closer to Logan Pass along Going-to-the-Sun Road. I would choose to stay at Rising Sun over the St. Mary Campground, but the St. Mary Campground accepts reservations, which is helpful as almost all of the campgrounds in the park fill nightly in the middle of the summer.

Rising Sun Campground

The Rising Sun Campground is halfway around St. Mary Lake, just west of St. Mary heading toward Logan Pass. Rising Sun is a beautiful place to camp, with Red Eagle Mountain as your main view. Rising Sun does not take reservations, so you will need to arrive early in the day to try to get a spot, as this campground does fill daily during the summer months.

The Rising Sun Campground is open from the middle of June through the middle of September. Some of the campsites here are in the open, and some provide more more shade thanks to surrounding forest. There are 84 campsites available, with several campsites being generator-free. There is potable water available throughout the campground, and the bathrooms have flush toilets and sinks with running water. The sinks are cold water without soap.

Next to the Rising Sun Campground you will conveniently find a camp store with gifts available, a casual restaurant, and a shower.

There are nightly ranger-led evening programs in the campground on various topics. Check the ranger-led activity schedule for the month you are visiting for the times. Bulletin boards in the campground will list each nightly topic.

Morning Eagle Falls

St. Mary Lake boat tours are available just across Going-to-the-Sun Road from the Rising Sun Campground.

Shuttle: Glacier's free shuttle system stops at the Rising Sun Campground. This is an excellent way to see Logan Pass, and not have to worry about parking.

St. Mary Campground (accepts reservations)

St. Mary Campground is the largest campground on the east side of the park. It is also one of only two campgrounds in Glacier that accepts reservations (along with Fish Creek). Reservations can be made at Reservations.gov.

There are 148 campsites available at the St. Mary Campground. The St. Mary Campground is open year-round, but during the winter months the campground operates in primitive status, and the camping is actually in the St. Mary picnic area.

My least favorite thing about this campground is that there is not a lot of shade. Usually we can leave our dogs in the camper during the day because it stays cool enough. Here most of the spots will be exposed to the sun. The other thing about this campsite is that you have to drive to get anywhere from here; it is not adjacent to any of the main lakes, hikes, or attractions in Glacier. However, being able to reserve a campsite on the east side of the Park is a big plus for the busy summer months.

You can purchase firewood in nearby St. Mary.

Shuttle: The free shuttle around Glacier National Park does not stop at the St. Mary Campground. The shuttle stops at the nearby St. Mary Visitor Center, so you will need to walk the short distance over to the visitor center to catch the shuttle.

Hotels and Lodging

St. Mary Lodge

The St. Mary Lodge is located just outside of the park's East St. Mary Entrance in the town of St. Mary at the intersection of Highway 89 and Going-to-the-Sun Road. This lodge has over a hundred guest rooms in six different facilities, leaving something to suit anyone's tastes from luxury suites to rustic lodges and motel rooms. The price for a room can be fairly inexpensive, to some of the most expensive in Glacier National Park, depending on the time of year and type of room.

The St. Mary Lodge has a restaurant known as the SnowGoose Grille, open throughout the summer. There are also a few other restaurant options in St. Mary. If you want to take lunch on the go, you can order the Box Lunch to pick up a sandwich and snacks to take with you on your day from the lobby. Call (406) 892-2525 for Box Lunch arrangements.

Rising Sun Motor Inn and Cabins

The Rising Sun Motor Inn is a great option for lodging along Going-to-the-Sun Road near St. Mary Lake on the east side of Glacier National Park. There are cottages and motor inn rooms available. The cabins are small and they are not fancy, but the Rising Sun is more affordable than a lot of places in the park. Cabins are less expensive than the Motor Inn rooms.

This location is also ideal for those on the east side of the Park who plan on visiting Logan Pass. Visiting Logan Pass is on my must-do list. The Rising Sun sits adjacent to the boat tours on St. Mary Lake, and the free park shuttle stops here. Here you will also find a restaurant, a camp store with basic snacks, and a gift shop.

View from Sun Point, photo courtesy of Blake Passmore

Bowman Lake

Chapter Eight: The North Fork, Bowman Lake, and Kintla Lake

The North Fork is a lesser-known section tucked away in the northwestern corner of Glacier National Park. The North Fork of the Flathead River marks the boundary of Glacier National Park on the west side of the park and flows from the Canadian border to meet the Middle Fork and the South Fork, and then flows past Columbia Falls and Kalispell into Flathead Lake. The North Fork of the Flathead River is designated a National Wild and Scenic River, protecting the free-flowing nature of the river from hydropower projects, in turn preserving the remarkable values of the river.

Much of the land surrounding the North Fork of the Flathead River is referred to as "the North Fork" by locals and visitors alike. The North Fork area is the less-traveled area of the park. This remote area in the northwest corner is a wonderful option for those looking to break away from the crowds elsewhere in the Park, and find serenity and stunning views that many Park visitors miss. The mountains, lakes, and meadows in this area are some of the most beautiful in all of Glacier, and perhaps, the world. We take several trips to this area each summer, stopping for baked goods at the Polebridge Mercantile and then driving up to spend time at the lakes. If you are looking to get into the wilderness and try paddleboarding or canoeing on a serene lake, the North Fork is the place for you. The North Fork is one of my favorite spots.

To get there, go west past Apgar and cross McDonald Creek, following the nicely paved Camas Road. About a ten minute drive will take you across the North Fork of the Flathead, the western boundary of the Park, and to the dusty, bumpy North Fork Road. The North Fork Road, which lies just outside of the Park, runs from Columbia Falls north to the Canadian border, although this border crossing is closed. A right turn will lead you to the tiny and popular small town of Polebridge. A left will take you to Columbia Falls. The road is not paved the entire way. From Polebridge, you can spend the day driving the bumpy roads to Bowman Lake and Kintla Lake, ideal for kayaking and paddle boarding.

> *NOTE: There is also the Inside North Fork Road that leads from beyond the Fish Creek Campground inside the park all the way up to the junction to Bowman Lake, bypassing the town of Polebridge, but this road is so frequently closed or partially closed due to annual flooding that I recommend going the longer way around using the North Fork Road.*

You will not have cell service or Internet access in the North Fork area of Polebridge, Bowman Lake, or Kintla Lake.

To fit the North Fork area into your schedule, you will want to set aside a day to explore, unless you plan on camping in the area. There are four campgrounds located in the North Fork: Bowman Lake, Kintla Lake, Quartz Creek and Logging Creek.

Several companies offer rafting trips down the North Fork of the Flathead River, including Glacier Raft Company and Glacier Guides. While there is the option of floating this river without a guide if you have a raft, I would not recommend it unless you are experienced. Wild and untouched, there is no dam to control water flow here. The water is high and rough during the spring and early summer, and can be dangerous to anyone who is not experienced. That being said, if you have any experience floating, you are free to float this beautiful river as you wish.

This less travelled area of Glacier will offer you wildlife, meadows, lakes, and beautiful panoramic views that are worth the small detour from Going-to-the-Sun Road and other popular areas of the Park. A nice view looking into the North Fork is seen from the tiny parking lot at the Forest and Fire Nature Trail (Huckleberry Trail) Trailhead just east of the junction of Camas road and North Fork Road.

North Fork of the Flathead River

Polebridge

The little town of Polebridge is the gateway to the Northwest Entrance of Glacier, providing access to Bowman and Kintla Lakes. Polebridge is one mile from the entrance, and is home to just a few people, as there is no electricity in this beautiful town. The community runs on solar panels and generator power.

You will want to get fuel before you leave Columbia Falls or West Glacier, because fuel prices are extravagant in Polebridge. You will not have cell service here, but there is a payphone available outside of the Polebridge Mercantile.

The Polebridge Mercantile and the Northern Lights Saloon (both powered by generators) are the main attraction here. You can't miss them as you enter Polebridge. The Polebridge Mercantile is fondly known as the "Merc," and is famous for its baked goods. Your kids will love this place, offering an array of sweet treats, including huckleberry macaroon cookies and huckleberry bearclaws. They also sell delicious sandwiches, and they do have ice for sale. You can find other limited groceries, gifts, and books for sale here. The Merc is open year-round, and has been serving this area for over 100 years.

> INSIDER'S TIP: If you don't make it to Polebridge, you can now find the Merc's baked goods at the Stumptown Marketplace in downtown Whitefish, Montana.

Polebridge Mercantile

The Northern Lights Saloon is next door to the Merc, and offers dinner, drinks, and live entertainment throughout the summer (from the end of May through the middle of September). This is a fun place to gather with outdoor picnic tables on the lawn and an outhouse in the rear, serving as the public restroom.

Polebridge has a number of accommodations that book up to a year in advance, so be sure to plan ahead. Keep in mind that there is no electricity in Polebridge, so be prepared to use outdoor bathrooms and to not have running water. The Merc offers cabins for rent that include a voucher for the Merc bakery for breakfast. There is also the North Fork Hostel, which may not be something you would choose with a family. You can view all accommodations and links to cabins outside of the Merc at polebridgemerc.com/stay.

Every year at noon on the Fourth of July, Polebridge has a fun patriotic parade. If you plan to attend, be sure to bring an umbrella for shade, a blanket, and a cooler with food and drinks so you don't have to wait in line, as this is a busy day in Polebridge.

Even if you just pass through Polebridge to reach Bowman Lake or Kintla Lake, be sure to swing into the Merc for some treats, and strike up a conversation with other travelers at the picnic tables outside of the Northern Lights Saloon.

The drive from Apgar to Polebridge takes about 45 minutes.

Bowman Lake

Bowman Lake is approximately 32 miles from the West Entrance of Glacier, and 6 miles from the town of Polebridge. This lake offers stunning mountain views similar to Lake McDonald, but the lake itself is smaller, and is the third largest lake in Glacier.
Bowman Lake is accessible by driving through Polebridge and re-entering the Park. The road from Polebridge to Bowman Lake is bumpy and winding, and therefore RV's, and truck and trailer combinations are not recommended. The road is also quite narrow and therefore you will want to take corners with caution of approaching vehicles. I have seen several cars test this road, but I would definitely recommend a higher clearance four-wheel drive vehicle.

North Fork with mountain views

Bowman Lake has a picnic area and a large beach area with a grassy section available for day visitors. Motorized vessels are permitted on Bowman Lake, but must be 10 horsepower or less. This lake is a perfect place to bring a canoe or kayak, and fisherman will enjoy this lake. There are several hikes that leave from Bowman Lake, including Quartz Lake Loop, but I do not recommend them on my family hiking lists because of length and elevation gain. If your time in Glacier is limited, choose some of the other hikes discussed.

Bowman Lake is a gem; I love to take my kayak and paddleboard to enjoy at sunset. The water is calm here most of the time, and you can't beat the views and fewer people. Bring mosquito repellent if you plan on visiting Bowman Lake, as the bugs can be bad at certain times of the year.

> TIP: If you visit Bowman Lake, be sure to follow the trail that leads toward Quartz Lake to your right from the boat launch area. Follow it for about five minutes until you reach the bridge that crosses over the outlet stream. You can walk down to the lake from this bridge, and this is a pretty spot.

Camping at Bowman Lake

Bowman Lake Campground has large campsites that are just a short walk down to Bowman Lake through the trees. Every site is in the trees, providing shade and privacy.

Bowman Lake has 48 campsites, all of which are first-come, first-serve, so you will want to arrive early in the day to get a site. You can also check the Campground Status page on the Park's website before departing from West Glacier or Apgar, as you will not have Internet access once you drive into the North Fork area or at Polebridge or Bowman Lake. That will tell you if the campground has filled for the day, and what time it has been filling in previous days.

Bowman Lake Campground is recommended as tent-only, because the road up has

Autumn colors at Bowman Lake

sharp turns and there is hardly enough room for two vehicles in a lot of places. I have seen people pull small campers up to the campground. The Bowman Lake Campground has some of the largest and nicest campsites I have seen inside of the park. If you are able to get a camper trailer up the bumpy road, you will easily fit it into these spacious camping sites.

The summer season runs from the end of May through the middle of September. Primitive camping is available from September through October. During primitive camping, water is not available and you have to bring your own drinking water.

Potable water from spigots is available throughout the campground, and there are pit toilets. There are no flush toilets or showers at this campground. Because RV's and trailers do not generally travel this road, there is no disposal station.

Kintla Lake

Kintla Lake is 40 miles from the West Entrance of Glacier in a remote section of the North Fork. Kintla Lake is slightly smaller than Bowman Lake, making it the fourth largest lake in Glacier. This is the most remote campground in the Park. You will drive through Polebridge, re-enter the Park using the Northwest Entrance, and proceed past the turn to Bowman Lake for another 14 miles until you reach the lake.

The drive from Polebridge to Kintla Lake is fairly level, and winds through open meadows paralleling the North Fork to your west and the peaks of Glacier to your east. Toward the last part of the drive, you will enter the forest and drive by beautiful streams. As with the rest of the North Fork, this is a bumpy dirt road, so RV's and truck and trailer combinations are not recommended. This drive is long, so set aside a day to travel to Kintla Lake to enjoy it, or plan on staying the night in the campground. The drive from Polebridge to Kintla Lake takes a little over an hour, depending on your speed tolerance on the bumpy road.

Kintla Lake has crystal clear water

Kintla Lake has a picnic area with pit toilets and picnic benches for day use. There is a small beach, significantly smaller than Bowman Lake, and very limited parking available close to the lake. Be sure to take a walk down the shore to the right and cross a foot bridge over the nice little stream leaving the lake.

No motorcraft is allowed on Kintla Lake. This makes the lake ideal for canoeing, kayaking, and standup paddle boarding. This is also a fantastic lake for trout fishing, and a good place to look for bears along the shoreline.

Camping at Kintla Lake

The Kintla Lake Campground is in the trees, but many campsites have views of the lake. There are only 13 campsites available, and there are no flush toilets, showers, or a disposal station. The campsites also tend to be small here, but the road is much smoother than the road to Bowman Lake, so if you can fit a small camper trailer into one of the camping sites, feel free to bring it.

Kintla Lake is open from the end of May to the middle of September. There is a hand pump available for potable water during the summer, and there are pit toilets available. Primitive camping is available from the middle of September to the end of October, when the nightly fee is reduced and there is no water available at this time, so be sure to bring drinking water during this time. We are in the habit of always packing our own water!

Bring a tent, food, water, and non-motorized watercraft, and enjoy your time at Kintla Lake. Most other visitors to Glacier miss it!

Kintla and Bowman Lakes are popular with kayakers

Hiking at Kintla Lake

You will not find good family friendly day hikes in this location. The hikes leaving from this point require that everyone in your party is up to hiking longer distances and able to spend a night in the backcountry. The Boulder Pass Trail travels along the north shores of Kintla Lake and Upper Kintla Lake, where you can continue over Boulder Pass to Goat Haunt, or connect back around to Bowman Lake.

Logging Creek and Quartz Creek Campgrounds

Logging Creek and Quartz Creek are on the Inside North Fork Road between Fish Creek Campground at Lake McDonald and Bowman Lake. Be sure to check the road status on the Inside North Fork Road before traveling, because it is often closed in sections due to annual flooding.

Both campgrounds are first-come, first-serve, but are less likely to fill throughout the summer and therefore can be used as backups if Bowman and Kintla Lake campgrounds are full when you arrive. Do not bring your RV or camper trailer to these campgrounds, because the dirt road is windy and bumpy. It is quicker to get to Logging Creek and Quartz Creek from Polebridge than by driving from the Fish Creek Campground.

Neither Quartz Creek nor Logging Creek has flush toilets, showers, or a disposal station. There are pit toilets available at each campground.

Quartz Creek is the smallest campground in Glacier, with only 7 sites available. The campground is in the trees, with no great views. Quartz Creek is considered a primitive campground because there is no water available, and is open from July to October.

From Quartz Creek, you can hike 6.2 miles one way down to Lower Quartz Lake for a pretty view, but this is not a hike I recommend for families because of the distance and the location. The lake is pretty, but there are not a lot of views along the ridge as you hike. Drive to Bowman Lake and enjoy that view without having to hike, or take some other shorter, more popular hikes – unless your primary goal is to really get away from the crowds.

Logging Creek is approximately 9 miles from Polebridge, and only has 7 campsites available. Logging Creek is open from July to September, and operates as a primitive campground all of the time because there is no water available. If you are looking for solitude, Logging Creek is a great choice, as not many people go here. The hike to Logging Lake begins near this campground, and although the Glacier Park website lists this as a "great family day hike," I don't recommend it as a "great family hike." There are many other beautiful, easy, less off-the-beaten-path hikes to enjoy with your family. Unless you plan on spending several weeks exploring every corner of the park, and want to camp overnight at Logging Lake, put this lower on your list of must-do hikes.

I would only camp at Quartz Creek or Logging Creek if you arrive at Bowman Lake or Polebridge and have nowhere to stay. Be sure to bring your own water, and a tent, if you plan on staying at these campgrounds.

Programs

There are no programs available in the North Fork region of Glacier National Park.

Nap time at Bowman Lake

Birch Lake in the Jewel Basin

Photo courtesy of Blake Passmore

Chapter Nine: Activities Outside of Glacier National Park

Glacier National Park is tucked away in the northwest corner of Montana. This popular area of the state located in the Rocky Mountains provides many opportunities for outdoor recreation, history, and family fun. There is plenty to do outside of Glacier National Park for families.

The two airports closest to Glacier National Park are Glacier International Airport and Great Falls International Airport. Glacier International, located in Kalispell, Montana, is about 30 minutes from the West Entrance of Glacier National Park. Great Falls International is 163 miles from the East Entrance at St. Mary, and will take you about 2.5 hours driving.

Two of the main entrances to Glacier are near the small towns of West Glacier and St. Mary. West Glacier is located at the West Entrance to Glacier National Park, and St. Mary is the east entry point to Glacier National Park. West Glacier and St. Mary are the starting points of Going-to-the-Sun Road.

There are three entrances on the east side the Park, including the Many Glacier Entrance, the St. Mary Entrance, and the Two Medicine Entrance. The town of East Glacier is near the Two Medicine Entrance. It will take you about an hour to drive between East Glacier and St. Mary.

Kalispell, Montana, is located in the Flathead Valley. The Flathead Valley, named for the Salish (Flathead) Indians, includes Flathead Lake and the popular resort towns of Whitefish and Bigfork. You might consider spending a few nights in Bigfork or Whitefish during your visit to Glacier, if time allows. Columbia Falls and Kalispell are also beautiful and hospitable towns, but do not have quite the same festive, tourist feel that Whitefish and Bigfork offer.

View of the Flathead Valley from Big Mountain

This chapter focuses on activities such as scenic lift rides, white water rafting, lakes, and golfing near both West Glacier and East Glacier. For more information on the towns, amenities, and the restaurants, see Chapter Five: West Glacier, Apgar, and Lake McDonald, and Chapter Six: East Glacier and Two Medicine.

Activities in West Glacier and the Flathead Valley

The following activities are located on the west side of Glacier National Park, near the West Entrance to Glacier National Park, within about 30 minutes drive from West Glacier, Montana.

Big Sky Waterpark

The Big Sky Waterpark is Montana's largest waterpark, located on Highway 2 in Columbia Falls. Open from June to August, this is a family-friendly activity on your trip that is sure to entertain children – and adults - for a day.

The waterpark offers waterslides, river rides, bumper cars, an antique carousel, mini-golf, picnic areas, and concession stands. You may bring your own food into the park.

Discounts are available for spectators – those that do not wish to use the slides but want to enter the park or supervise young children in the wading pool.

You can find more information at **bigskywp.com**.

House of Mystery

The House of Mystery is located along Highway 2 between Columbia Falls and Hungry Horse on your way to Glacier. The House of Mystery is not far from the Big Sky Waterpark, and has been here since I was a child. This is agreat adventure for exploring with young children

Flyfishing on the Flathead River
Photo courtesy of Blake Passmore

This tour is led by a guide through a series of attractions based on the power of the "vortex" located at the site. The actual "House of Mystery" is a shack located in the woods that has slanted walls and ceilings that at the very least make for some fun photo opportunities. Another highlight is the "Platform." Standing on one end of the "Platform" will make you "shrink" four to six inches, while standing on the other end you will be your normal size. You will also spend time learning about your "aura."

Each tour is about one hour. The House of Mystery is open from April until the second week in October. Kids under five are free.

You can find out more information at **montanavortex.com**.

Glacier Zip Line Adventures

Located next to the House of Mystery at 7840 Highway 2 East in Columbia Falls, the Glacier Zip Line Adventures and its tall platform is clearly visible on your way to Glacier. Eight zip lines take you through the trees, with the option of a shorter course for anyone who doesn't want to go the whole route. The Glacier Zip Line was established in 2015, and is open daily during the summer.

You can find more information at **glacier-ziplines.com**.

Huckleberry/Cherry Stands

A highlight of your trip to Montana might include enjoying huckleberries or Flathead Lake Cherries. You will find huckleberry-themed products and food throughout Glacier and the Flathead Valley.

Huckleberry stands and cherry stands are also found just outside Glacier in Coram and Hungry Horse. You will also find Flathead Lake Cherry stands in surrounding areas near Bigfork and along Flathead Lake.

You can pick your own huckleberries along the trails in Glacier, or anywhere you can find them. Visitors to Glacier can pick one quart of huckleberries per person per day.

There is also the option of picking your own cherries at a cherry orchard on Flathead Lake. There are a few options for picking along both the East and West shores of the lake.

You can find more information about picking your own cherries at: **montanavacationblog.com**.

Glacier Highline

The Glacier Highline opened on Highway 2 East in Coram in 2015, and is an outdoor aerial adventure park. This is for the thrill seeker, featuring 29 activities at varying heights in the treetops. This adventure is open daily throughout the summer months. There is also a playground on site for anyone traveling with children too small to participate. The Glacier Highline is fun for anyone looking to get a workout and defy gravity in the treetops. Book a trip in advance or walk-in.

Visit **glacierhighline.com** for more information.

Amazing Fun Center

The Amazing Fun Center is a fun activity center located just 7 miles west of West Glacier, on Highway 2. This center includes mini-golf, Go Karts, bumper boats, bank shot basketball, and a large maze.

There is something for the entire family here. A family could spend an entire day doing the activities. The Center opens Memorial Day weekend and closes weekdays after September 1. They are open the first three weekends in September. They offer pricing for individual activities or for a full day pass to partake in all activities. Children under five are free.

You can find more information at **amazingfuncenter.com**.

Glacier Distilling, Coram, Montana

Glacier Distilling is known for its variety of whiskeys that you can try in their whiskey barn in Coram, Montana. Their spirits, a tribute to the region, include Glacier Dew, Wheatfish Whiskey, Bad Rock Rye, North Fork Whiskey, and Fireweed Bourbon. There are many other beverages available with an outdoor seating area. The bright red barn can't be missed as you are driving toward Glacier National Park from Columbia Falls and Hungry Horse. Parents, this is right next door to the Amazing Fun Center.

More information can be found at **glacierdistilling.com**.

Glacier Distilling

The Huckleberry Patch, Hungry Horse, Montana

The Huckleberry Patch is a gift shop and huckleberry food store located in Hungry Horse, Montana. Conveniently on your way to West Glacier, this is a great place to stop for a huckleberry gift, huckleberry pancakes, or huckleberry ice cream.

Their huckleberries are hand picked and processed without any artificial flavoring. You can buy jams, syrups, and pies year-round directly from their website. They will even ship you a huckleberry pie. I love to stop and enjoy a huckleberry shake on my way home from Glacier.

More information can be found at **huckleberrypatch.com**.

Whitefish Mountain Resort Summer Activities

Whitefish Mountain Resort at Big Mountain is just north of Whitefish, Montana, and offers a variety of summer activities that are worth doing while visiting the Flathead Valley. From hiking, to scenic lift rides, aerial parks, and alpine sliding, the resort has something for everyone in the family. The following activities are open throughout the summer, but only Friday through Sunday in September.

Alpine Slide at Whitefish Mountain Resort

Join in the fun at the Alpine Slide daily throughout the summer. You will ride in a sled and control your own speed around the turns down a section of the mountain. This is similar to a bobsled without the ice, and is a great activity for younger children; anyone aged 1 and up is allowed to ride. Children under 48 inches who share a sled with an adult who have purchased a ticket may ride for free. Note that this does not always operate if it is raining. Follow the signs to buy your tickets and begin the slide at the base of Chair 1.

Riding the chair lift or gondola on a scenic lift ride to the Summit of Whitefish Mountain Resort is a wonderful activity for the entire family. Food and drinks are available in the

Summit House when you reach the top, and the views of the Flathead Valley during the ride and from the top are incredible. The view from the backside looks into the peaks of Glacier and Canada. Open daily in the summer, the mountain offers one-way tickets if you want to hike one way and ride the other.

The Zip Line is a popular tour where you hang from a harness and fly down several cables, and you can race the person next to you. You can choose between the five-zip or the seven-zip line tour. It is recommended to call ahead to make a reservation.

For ages 7 and up, the Aerial Adventure Park offers some daring adventures. Known as the "obstacle course in the trees," the aerial adventure park has five courses varying from easy to difficult. You don't need any experience to join in on the fun. You will be strapped in a harness, and climb on nets, bridges, trapezes, ladders, zip lines, and similar obstacles. Be ready to be 10-50 feet off the ground and wear closed toe shoes. (Not recommended for pregnant women.)

The "Summit Nature Center" is located on the lower level of the Summit House, located at the top of Whitefish Mountain Resort. Here families can join a Forest Service Naturalist on a free nature walk in July and August to learn about Montana's alpine ecosystem. Children ages 7 – 11 can become Junior Forest Rangers, by completing an activity book, and they will be given an official badge and certificate. Families can also borrow an Outdoor Adventure Pack with field guides and materials that help families explore outside without taking a guided tour.

The "Spider Monkey Mountain" is for children 34 inches and 4 years and up that want to climb their way up the webbed tower and down a giant slide.

The Danny On Trail is a 3.8-mile (one way) hiking trail that switchbacks up the mountain, around to the backside, and up to the Summit House, where you can ride the lift back down for a fee. This is not an easy trail; it gains 2,434 feet in elevation. The first few miles going up are very pretty, as you cross over the ski runs and have panoramic views of the Flathead Valley through open fields of wildflowers. The last part of the hike is in the trees. I sometimes like to ride the lift to the top (for a fee), and then hike the trail down. I hiked this trail a lot as a young child, but there are some steep sections closer to the top where you want to watch small children. The last two miles of the Danny On trail (at the highest elevation) are excellent for huckleberry picking, so be sure to bring a bag if you want to collect more than you can eat!

Whitefish Mountain Resort also has a Mountain Bike Park. Catch the chair lift up from June until September and ride your bike down. The mountain boasts 27 miles of trails for riding, including advanced terrain. Rent a bike and all equipment you need (helmets are required) from Snow Ghost Outfitters at the base of the mountain. The mountain does sell season passes, or day passes.

The "Walk in the Treetops" is a daily 2 ½ hour nature walk on a boardwalk through the treetops, with water and snacks provided. Wear closed toe shoes and learn about the local plants and animals. Call Whitefish Mountain Resort to make a reservation.

Of course, if you visit during the winter months, Whitefish Mountain Resort at Big Mountain offers skiing, snowboarding, snowmobiling, and cross country skiing. I grew up skiing at "Big Mountain," as it was called then. This is an awesome mountain to ski, and has plenty of beginner and intermediate slopes for young children, and a lot of steep and deep to keep the adults busy.

Learn more at **skiwhitefish.com**.

Bigfork Summer Playhouse

The Bigfork Summer Playhouse is a popular theatre by the bay located at the northeast end of Flathead Lake in downtown Bigfork, Montana. The playhouse features a variety of new plays each year, and makes for a fun night out in the Flathead Valley. There are often plays that children would also enjoy.

The Bigfork Summer Playhouse also teams up with a few local restaurants to offer a package deal of 2 show tickets and dinner prior to attending the theater. Call the playhouse for specific information.

Bigfork Summer Playhouse

For more information: bigforksummerplayhouse.com.

Raceway Park

Every Saturday night at Raceway Park during the summer, you can find many locals watching cars race around an asphalt oval track. This can be a fun event for the family, but you might want to consider earplugs for younger children, as the races are loud. Located at 3790 Highway 93 North, between Kalispell and Whitefish, Montana.

More information is found at montanaracewaypark.com.

Rodeos at the Majestic Valley Arena and the Blue Moon Night Club

What better way to enjoy Montana with your family than attending a rodeo? If you are looking to enjoy a true Montana rodeo on your trip, the Flathead Valley offers a few options.

The Majestic Valley Arena is between Kalispell and Whitefish on Highway 93 . This indoor arena offers year-round family-friendly events, including rodeos throughout the summer.

For more information about events here, visit majesticvalleyarena.com.

The Blue Moon Rodeo is offered several evenings throughout the summer at the Blue Moon Night Club just west of Columbia Falls, Montana. This is a popular local event that lasts about two hours and has bull riding, barrel racing, and roping. This is a great way to spend a nice Montana summer evening.

Check here for the current schedule: bluemoonmontana.com/rodeo.htm.

Helicopter Tours

Glacier Heli Tours located in West Glacier offers one-hour tours in helicopters over Glacier. Children are welcome on these tours.

The tour takes you around the entire park, flying up the east side of the Continental Divide to Waterton Park and then down the west side of the Continental Divide back to West Glacier. Headsets are provided, and you will be given brief commentary from the pilot.

> TIP: Make your reservation a few days in advance. That way you are not only guaranteed there is room for your tour, but then you have a chance of adding other people to your trip in order to save money.

For information on booking a helicopter tour, visit glacierhelitours.net.

Rafting the Flathead River
Photo courtesy of Glacier Guides
and Montana Raft Company

White Water Rafting

There are several private companies that offer white water rafting just outside the Park in West Glacier. Most companies offer trips on either the Middle Fork or the North Fork of the Flathead River. Both rivers are clean and beautiful. You can choose from full or half-day white water rafting trips, dinner trips, multi-day trips, and inflatable kayak trips. Keep in mind that most rafting trips are for children ages 6 and up, although some scenic trips allow children starting at 18 months. Trips will get longer as the year goes on, because the water gets lower and makes the water slower. Plan on getting wet, so wear appropriate clothing.

Glacier Guides

Glacier Guides is 1.5 miles west of West Glacier on Highway 2, and offers rafting, hiking, and fishing trips with lodging available. They have several family-friendly rafting trips to choose from. For children ages 3 and up, they offer a mellow "Scenic Float Trip" for 2 hours down the Middle Fork. Enjoy whitewater trips down the Middle Fork. Their two-day wilderness float on the North Fork with an overnight stay at the Polebridge Hostel is a popular option. Glacier Guides also offers custom options and inflatable kayaks. All trips leave from their office on Highway 2.

Contact them for more information at **glacierguides.com**.

Glacier Raft Company

Glacier Raft Company offers rafting, fly fishing, and lodging. For their raft and fishing trips, you can find their office in the heart of West Glacier. They offer a "Half-day Whitewater," or a "Half-day Whitewater with Riverside Dinner" along the Middle Fork. The "Half Day Scenic Float" is a relaxing way to see the beauty of the river. There is also the option of the "Full Day Whitewater with Riverside Lunch," full of rapids and a barbeque lunch along the river.

For more information, visit **glacierraftco.com**.

Glacier Raft Company also offers lodging near West Glacier at the Glacier Outdoor Center at 12400 US Highway 2. From personal experience, these cabins are new, homey, and a great option for large families or groups traveling together to stay near West Glacier. The views from this property are spectacular, looking into Glacier National Park and the North Fork. On the property there is also a pavilion that is a great option for weddings, and four stocked trout ponds for kids to fish.

Great Northern Resort

The Great Northern Resort

The Great Northern Resort is located just a mile west of West Glacier on Highway 2, and offers rafting and lodging. Choose from whitewater rafting, scenic floats, and dinner trips. Half day and full day raft trips are available. There is also the option of dinner trips on either the scenic or whitewater floats. Scenic floats are great for ages 3 and up. I have been rafting with them several times throughout the years, and their trips will not disappoint!

We have stayed here and their cabins are a nice option for groups traveling to the area. The cozy cabins overlook a pond and the mountains, and you will depart from here if you book a rafting trip.

For more information, visit **glacierparkraft.com**.

Wild River Adventures

Wild River Adventures is another company in West Glacier that offers custom raft trips, dinner trips, scenic floats, whitewater rafting trips, and multi-day trips.

Lion Lake near Hungry Horse, MT

Visit **riverwild.com** for more information.

Horseback Rides/ Swan Mountain Outfitters

Horseback riding is a fun activity for a family that enjoys horses, or doesn't want to do much hiking. Swan Mountain Outfitters offers a trail ride through the mountains leaving from West Glacier, just outside of the west entrance to Glacier National Park. While not their most scenic trip, this is a great option for anyone looking to ride a horse near Glacier National Park.

There are many chances to ride the horses with Swan Mountain Outfitters inside of the Park as well.

Horseback rides

For more information on horseback rides within Glacier National Park, see Chapter Two.

Glacier View Golf Course (West Glacier)

Glacier View Golf Course is located in West Glacier, so the proximity to the park is a plus for anyone wanting to golf. This is a short course at a par 69, and a Family Tee Concept used for junior golfers. There are also many other opportunities for golf in nearby Whitefish, Columbia Falls, and Kalispell.

Lake Five and Lake Five Resort

Lake Five is a pretty mountain lake just four miles from the West Entrance to Glacier. The Lake Five Resort in particular is a fun place to go with kids, because they have a beach with floating docks that have slides, as well as volleyball

Loving life at Lake Five

courts. They do charge a day use fee to use their beach access if you are not staying with them. The Lake Five Resort also has cabins and camping available, and the camping sites are always booked. Camp spots are much more expensive than inside of Glacier National Park, but you do get the use of the swimming area, and they do allow pets for an additional daily fee.

Find out more at **lakefiveresort.com**.

Whitefish City Beach

The town of Whitefish is located on Whitefish Lake, only 30 minutes from the West Entrance to Glacier. Whitefish Lake is a pretty 7-mile long lake that provides views of Whitefish Mountain Resort at Big Mountain. The easiest public access to Whitefish Lake is at the Whitefish City Beach.

Whitefish City Beach is a nice swimming area

City Beach provides a large sandy beach area, a roped swimming area, docks, and picnic tables. Lifeguards are on duty during busy periods, and there are limited food and refreshments for sale during the summer. There is also a public boat dock, and canoes and paddleboats are available to rent.

Whitefish City Beach is popular because it is so close to town. However, if you don't have a desire to only swim in the heat of the day, mornings and evenings are beautiful and often completely deserted, even in the middle of summer. It is still warm enough to swim late into the evening, as long as you can get past the initial chill when you jump in! Head down to watch the beautiful summer sunsets.

Sunset at the Whitefish Lake Lodge

Getting there: Take Highway 93 to Whitefish. Turn left onto Baker Avenue, and go north, through downtown and over the viaduct. Turn left onto Edgewood Drive at the light just past the viaduct. Follow Edgewood for ½ mile to the entrance to City Beach. You will see a sign pointing you where to turn to reach the parking lot.

Flathead Lake: Lakeside, Bigfork, Wayfarers State Park, and The Raven

Volunteer Park on Flathead Lake

Flathead Lake is the largest natural freshwater lake west of the Mississippi River. It is 27.3 miles long and up to 15.5 miles wide. Tours of Flathead Lake are available on the west side departing daily on the Far West Boat Tours.

Lakeside is a small town on the West Shore of the lake, with a few restaurants, and access to Blacktail Mountain Ski Resort. Lakeside also has Volunteer Park, a beautiful grassy park located on Flathead Lake with docks for swimming.

On the northeast shore of Flathead Lake, you will find the town of Bigfork. Although Flathead Lake has several state parks, Wayfarers State Park is conveniently located just outside of Bigfork. There is camping, a public boat launch, and plenty of spots to swim. Way-

Wayfayers State Park on Flathead Lake

farers is a great spot for young children because it starts out shallow for wading. There are also plenty of cliffs for older children and adults to jump off of into the lake. The Raven restaurant is located on Flathead Lake just south of Bigfork, and an outdoor deck and patio make this a fantastic place to be for sunset.

Bigfork also has several nice art galleries, shops, and restaurants, and is definitely worth a stop on your way to Glacier National Park. The Marina Cay Resort is a great place to stay on Flathead Lake, and has a Tiki Bar open on weekends throughout the summer.

Hungry Horse Dam/ Reservoir

The Hungry Horse Dam and the Hungry Horse Reservoir are located just 15 miles south of the West Entrance to Glacier and West Glacier. This concrete arch dam is located on the South Fork of the Flathead River, and is 564 feet high. Hungry Horse Reservoir is 34 miles long with beautiful views from its west shores of Great Northern Mountain. The Reservoir is a fantastic place for swimming, fishing, boating, and camping. Here you will find cutthroat trout, bull trout, and whitefish. If you have a boat, this is a great place for island camping.

Lower St. Mary Lake near Babb, MT
Photo courtesy of Blake Passmore

East Glacier, St. Mary, and Babb Activities

The following activities are located on the east side of Glacier National Park, near the towns of Babb, St. Mary, and East Glacier.

Glacier Park Golf Club

The Glacier Park Golf Club is a nine-hole, par 36, golf course located at the historic Glacier Park Lodge in East Glacier, Montana. This public course is open from May to September, and offers the eastern front of Glacier National Park as the backdrop. Located within the boundary of the Blackfeet Indian Reservation, all 9 holes are named after former chiefs of the Blackfeet Nation. This is the oldest golf greens golf course in Montana. Carts and club rentals are available. Call ahead to reserve a tee time.

For the entire family, the Glacier Park Golf Club also sports a par 27 Pitch 'n Putt course that is a small fee and includes a Glacier Park Lodge souvenir ball. This is inexpensive and fun for all as you chip your way around the course that circles the Glacier Park Lodge!

You can find more information at **glacierparkinc.com**.

Museum of the Plains Indian

The Museum of the Plains Indian is located at the junction of Highway 2 and Highway 89 West in Browning, Montana. Browning is 13 miles east of East Glacier. The Museum is free from October to May, and is closed on all Federal holidays. From June to September, there is a small entry fee, and children under 6 are free. Visit the museum for exhibits and paintings featuring the Native American craftspeople and artists.

Glacier County Honey Company

For all the honey lovers, Glacier County Honey Company is a family-owned business that keeps bees, extracts and sells honey, and makes beeswax candles and ornaments for sale. This sweet company is found in Babb, Montana, not far from St. Mary on the east side of Glacier National Park, and you can find their honey at various retailers in northwest Montana, including the Lake McDonald Lodge and the Many Glacier Hotel.

The Honey Company offers an open house once per year when they sell wholesale honey to the public. Check their website for dates. They also offer private tours of the facilities on request from July to September, for opportunities to witness the honey extraction.

Contact them at **glaciercountyhoney.com**.

Snowshoeing in Glacier National Park near Marias Pass
Photo courtesy of Blake Passmore

Chapter Ten:
Winter in Glacier National Park

Most of this book has explored what there is for families to do in Glacier National Park during the summer months of June to September. However, Glacier Park is open year-round, and there is no reason not to visit if you have the chance to visit during the winter. This chapter explores some things to do during the months of October to May.

Ranger-Led Activities

In the winter months, there is a ranger-led snowshoe walk leaving from Apgar near West Glacier, Montana. Ranger-led snowshoe walks are offered on Saturdays and Sundays from the middle of January until the middle of March. Meet at the Apgar Visitor Center located near Apgar. The two-hour walk will look for wildlife and discuss plants and animals in the park during the winter months.

The snowshoe walk is free, but does require snowshoes if there is snow on the ground. You can bring your own snowshoes, or rent a pair from the Apgar Visitor Center for a few dollars. Eddie's in the Apgar Village also rents snowshoes, but they are more expensive than the Visitor Center. While the Park Service says this is not recommended for children under age 6, this is a very easy walk on level ground through the forest. We put our small children in backpack carriers and bring them along.

Winter Activities

Before partaking in winter activities in Glacier, stop at a ranger station for information on the weather and snow conditions.

Snowshoeing and Cross-Country Skiing

In addition to the ranger-led snowshoe walk, you can take your own snowshoes or rent and go for walks and hikes on your own.

There are cross-country ski trails throughout the park. Trails are found in Apgar, Lake McDonald, North Fork, St. Mary, Two Medicine, and Marias Pass. Visit **home.nps.gov/applications/glac/ski/xcski.htm** for more information on the area trails. These trails can also be used for hiking and snowshoeing.

Skiing at Whitefish Mountain Resort

Most of the ski routes are not marked, and you may have to break your own trail on less popular routes. The trails around Apgar are likely to be more heavily traveled if you do not want to break trail. Remember to keep snowshoes and ski tracks separate on the trail.

Snowmobiles are not permitted and pets are not allowed on trails.

Be sure to register at the trailhead registration box before leaving the trailhead.

Backcountry Skiing

I would recommend backcountry skiing in Glacier only for experts. The Izaak Walton Inn in Essex offers guided snowshoe and backcountry skiing trips. The Inn also offers cross-country ski lessons.

Go to **izaakwaltoninn.com** for more information.

For information on avalanches before backcountry skiing, be sure to check **flatheadavalanche.org/**.

Winter Road Status

Once the snow falls on Glacier, the park does not maintain all of the roads. Unplowed roads make the majority of Glacier Park inaccessible to vehicles from the middle of December until spring. eleven miles of Going-to-the-Sun Road and Apgar Village is plowed in the winter on the west side, and about a mile and a half on the east side is all that is plowed in the winter.

Making tracks
Photo courtesy of Blake Passmore

On the west side, you are generally able to drive from Apgar to the Lake McDonald Lodge, following Going-to-the-Sun Road around Lake McDonald.

It is critical to understand that you cannot drive over Logan Pass during the winter months. Logan Pass is the pass that you drive over on Going-to-the-Sun Road that connects West Glacier to St. Mary. There is too much snow over the pass in the winter, so you will not be able to drive the entire Going-to-the-Sun Road in the winter months. Do not count on being able to drive to Logan Pass until the end of June or the beginning of July, depending on the snowfall each year.

You can check the current road status by visiting **nps.gov/glac**.

Hotels and Camping – Where to Stay in the Winter

The hotels in Glacier close during the winter. Because there are a lot less visitors during the winter, the hotels board up and close down until the spring. If you are looking for a hotel, you will want to look in nearby Whitefish, Kalispell, or Columbia Falls. Whitefish has a particularly festive atmosphere over the holidays and the winter.

Car camping is available in at the Apgar Picnic Area and St. Mary Campground for free. There is nowhere to plug in and there are no bathrooms or other services available.

If you want to backcountry camp, backcountry permits are free during the winter months. Permits are required to camp in the backcountry. Park Headquarters are open during the week in the winter months near West Glacier, and the Apgar Visitor Center is open weekends during the winter.

Visit **nps.gov/glac/planyourvisit/backcountry.htm** for information on obtaining a permit.

Glacier National Park from Whitefish Mountain Resort

Lake McDonald in a wintery mood

Ousel Creek near Glacier National Park
Photo courtesy of Blake Passmore

Chapter Eleven:
Know Before You Go

Glacier Park, also called the "Crown of the Continent," is a treasure trove of fascinating animals, geology, history, and characters. This chapter covers some basic information as far as plants, camping, and hiking that are not covered in each particular chapter of the book.

Also, be sure to check out the Glacier Institute, discussed in Chapter Two.

Huckleberries, Plants, and Wildflowers

Glacier National Park is full of wildflowers, and July and August are the best time to see the alpine flowers, including Bear Grass, Paintbrush, and the Glacier Lily. But remember, picking wildflowers is illegal inside of Glacier.

Glacier is also famous for its huckleberries, a tart wild berry that is similar to a blueberry. You will find huckleberries all over Glacier, particularly along hiking trails at higher elevations. You can pick huckleberries in Glacier. Visitors are allowed to pick one quart per person per day for personal consumption. Bring a container with you so that you can take some home with you. If your primary goal is collecting huckleberries, I recommend you bring a hard plastic container with a lid if you can carry it. I carry a few Ziploc bags for berry storage. We tend to eat most of what we pick while on the trail, but you could save yours to eat later or for baking.

You can also buy huckleberries from local stands between Hungry Horse and West Glacier, and huckleberry products are sold around and throughout Glacier. The Huckleberry Patch in Hungry Horse is a great place to buy huckleberry-everything.

Huckleberries usually are in full force in late July to mid-August. Remember that grizzly bears feed on huckleberries, so be careful and keep an eye out while picking!

Fuel

Finding fuel for your vehicle can be difficult while traveling in and around Glacier. You cannot get gas anywhere inside of the park. Be sure to keep your gas tank near full, as it may take awhile to find the next gas station.

Enjoying a hidden waterfall

You will be able to fuel your vehicle near park entrances in East Glacier, West Glacier, and St. Mary. You will also be able to get gas in Babb, just outside of Many Glacier. You can also get gas in Polebridge, located in the North Fork, but you may pay up to double the price of a regular tank of gas, so I recommend filling up elsewhere. Fuel is also available in Browning, Hungry Horse, Coram, Columbia Falls, and Whitefish.

Cell service

You will not have cell phone service in most areas inside of the park. There is no cell service at Many Glacier, Two Medicine, the North Fork including Polebridge, or Logan Pass. You should be able to get cell service in West Glacier, East Glacier, St. Mary, and Babb. There is also cell service at Apgar Village just inside the west entrance at Lake McDonald. You can get a little service at Fish Creek Campground along Lake McDonald.

Look for beargrass on your hikes

Camping

Camping is an affordable way to travel with the entire family. There are thirteen campgrounds available in Glacier Park. Some of the campgrounds only allow tent camping. You will find information on the campgrounds available in each specific area by chapter.

For general information on Glacier National Park's campgrounds,
visit **nps.gov/glac/planyourvisit/camping.htm**.

Campground Operating Dates and Hookup Information

Campground operating dates vary by campground. If you happen to visit during the winter, the St. Mary Campground and the Apgar Picnic Area are open for camping, and there is no fee for camping from December 1st through March 31st.

If a campground is listed as "primitive status," it means that there are no flush toilets or potable water. This is the case at many campsites in the spring and fall.

None of the campgrounds in the Park have "full-hookups," but there are several private campgrounds just outside the Park with hookups available.

First-Come / First-Serve and Site Information

Keep in mind that most campgrounds in the park are first-come / first-serve. The exceptions are Fish Creek, St. Mary, and half of the group sites at Apgar (Many Glacier accepts reservations for a few sites starting in 2016). To reserve a site at Fish Creek, St. Mary and the Apgar group sites, call 1-877-444-6777, or reserve online at **recreation.gov/**. You can reserve these sites up to 6 months in advance, which is highly recommended. You must reserve at least 3 days ahead of your arrival in order to book a reservation.

Glacier National Park offers a "**Current Campground Status**" page at **home.nps.gov/applications/glac/cgstatus/cgstatus.cfm**.

If you are outside of the park and are able to access the Internet, this website will tell you whether the campground you are looking for is currently open to campers, and if it has filled for the night. To plan ahead, watch what time of the day a particular campground has filled recently, and be sure to arrive at the campsite before that time. You can also look at the fill times of each campground for each date in past years. I have also listed tips for each area in each respective chapter. I check this website multiple times a week, and always before leaving to find a campsite in the park.

When you arrive, even if the sign at the campground entry states that it is "full," it is still worth driving through to check for open sites. This is particularly true in the morning hours, when some campers may have left, but the sign may not have been updated yet.

At the Fish Creek and St. Mary campgrounds (where reservations are accepted), you will be checked in at a kiosk upon entry. At all other campsites (the ones that are first-come, first-serve), it is up to you to drive around and find an empty site.

For the first-come / first-serve sites, you will stop at a fee station (there are a few located in each campground) and get a fee envelope before driving through to look for a campsite. As you drive through looking for a spot, you will notice that the occupied sites have tags hanging from the site sign. The tags should have the date that the current party is leaving written on it, courtesy of the campground host. This is helpful to know which parties are leaving, and what sites will be opening up in the next few days.

Once you choose your site, tear off the top of the slip and hang it from your site sign. Be sure to return your fee envelope back to the fee station within 30 minutes of choosing your spot.

No Refund Policy

Glacier National Park campgrounds do not issue refunds. So be sure to only pay for the nights you know you will be staying. We usually only pay for two nights at a time, until we are sure we want to stay more nights. Poor weather may make you want to change campgrounds, so keep that in mind before paying.

Moose at Fishercap Lake

Biker/ Hiker Campsites

A few campsites at Apgar, Fish Creek, Avalanche, Many Glacier, Rising Sun, Two Medicine and St. Mary campgrounds are reserved for those on bicycles or hiking. This means that you can't have a motorized vehicle with you. Motorcycles must use a regular campsite. The biker/hiker campsites can hold up to 8 people per site. Each campground has a small per person fee for these sites.

Group Sites

There are group sites available for 9 to 24 campers. Five of Apgar Campground's ten group sites can be reserved up to one year in advance, and the other five are on a first-come/first-serve basis. St. Mary Campground has two group sites that can be reserved up to a year in advance. Many Glacier and Two Medicine campgrounds each have 1 group site, but these are only available on a first-come/first-serve basis.

Showers

Anyone (even non-campers) can pay to use the showers at the Rising Sun and Swiftcurrent campstores. The St. Mary and Fish Creek campgrounds have free token operated showers that are only for campers staying at those campgrounds, but the water may not always be warm. You can also find private campgrounds outside of the park that sell shower service. Ask a campground host for information on nearby showers outside of the park.

Generator Use

Utility hook-ups are not provided, so you may want to bring a generator. Each campground has specific times that generators can be used, and specific sites in some campgrounds do not allow generator use at all. Be sure to check current with a campground host if you have questions.

Firewood

Firewood is available for purchase at most camp stores. Gathering or cutting firewood is only allowed in a few specific areas. See each chapter for specific campground information.

Camping Regulations

Glacier has many regulations that apply to their campgrounds. You can obtain a list of regulations at the visitor centers in the Park, or at each respective campground. You can download the regulations here: **nps.gov/glac/planyourvisit/camping.htm**.

HERE ARE A FEW SIGNIFICANT REGULATIONS:

- There are specific food storage regulations to ensure that bears are not attracted to your food, trash, and the campgrounds. You can be fined for leaving out food. Be sure to always store all food away in a vehicle, camper, or the provided food storage containers located around the campgrounds when not being immediately consumed.
- You may only camp in designated areas.
- Sites may not be left unattended for more than 24 hours.
- A maximum of 8 people and two cars is permitted in each campsite.
- A maximum of two tents is allowed in each site.

- Group sites are for 9 or more people.
- Dogs are allowed in the campgrounds, but not on trails, and you are required to pick up after your pet. Bags are provided.
- From July 1 to Labor Day, camping is limited to 14 nights.
- All wastewater, including water from showers and dishwashing, must be contained, and disposed of in utility sinks or at RV dump stations provided at each campground.
- No fireworks allowed inside the Park.

Hiking

So many visitors drive Going-to-the-Sun Road, snap a few photos at the major pullouts, and leave Glacier Park missing out on so many amazing opportunities that can be easily enjoyed. Do not be afraid to step out of your vehicle. Glacier offers many easy trails for visitors to enjoy, leaving an option for any family to get out and enjoy some sights not far off the road. Trails such as Running Eagle Falls and Trail of the Cedars are even stroller and wheelchair accessible.

I have listed elevation gain for reference on the hikes in this book. These are approximate, as many websites have different elevation gains listed, and the National Park Service seems to vary from all of these. The elevation gains listed in this book are taken from **hikinginglacier.com**.

Each of the hikes discussed in the book are organized according to different sections of the Park. Each one offers something unique, so if you can make time to do more than one, I highly recommend it. I have specifically noted features that are important for those hiking with children: lakes, waterfalls, exposure to the elements, elevation, distance, and parking.

Mountain goats

I have noticed that my kids particularly like hiking to places where they will see animals, or have the chance to see waterfalls or play in lakes. Overlooks and views are not usually as popular with my small children, so this may be something to keep in mind when you are considering which hikes are best for you and your family.

Guided Hiking in Glacier National Park

Glacier National Park offers many free, guided tours for different hikes throughout the park. Be sure to check the Ranger-Led Activity Schedule for the area you want to hike, and see what is available.

Glacier Guides is the only company authorized to provide backpacking trips in Glacier National Park. You can find out more about this great local company by visiting their website at **glacierguides.com**.

Backcountry Permits

A backcountry permit is required in Glacier for all backcountry camping sites. For information and educational videos regarding camping in the Glacier backcountry, visit: **nps.gov/glac/planyourvisit/backcountry.htm**.

There are many backcountry sites that would be great to visit with children, and would make a day hike shorter by only having to hike one way each day. For example, Upper Two Medicine Lake Campground in the Two Medicine area would be a relatively easy way for a family with children to hike in and experience backcountry overnight camping.

Fireweed above Flathead Valley

You may gather firewood in backcountry campgrounds that allow wood fires.

Visitor Centers

There are three visitor centers located in Glacier National Park. There is the Apgar Visitor Center, the St. Mary Visitor Center, and the Logan Pass Visitor Center. The visitor center hours vary by time of year and location. There is also the Park Headquarters, located between Apgar and West Glacier.

You can visit **nps.gov/glac/planyourvisit/hours.htm** for up-to-date information on specific dates and operating hours for the entire park.

Entry Fees

Glacier National Park charges an entrance fee to enter the park boundaries. Visitors can purchase a single vehicle pass that is valid for 7 days, or a Glacier National Park Pass that remains valid for one year. There is also a 7-day pass available for those entering the park via motorcycle, bicycle, or on foot.

Another option is to purchase the **America the Beautiful, National Parks and Federal Recreational Lands Pass**, providing access to all national parks in the USA for one year.

Note: Waterton Lakes National Park has separate entrance fees.

Each year, national parks offer occasional fee-free days. On these days, entrance fees are waived and you can enter national parks for free.

The usual free dates are as follows: Martin Luther King Jr. Day, President's Day Weekend, First Weekend of National Park Week, August 25 (the National Park Service birthday), Public Lands Day, and Veteran's Day.

Park Regulations

Glacier National Park has many park regulations, but here are a few of the significant ones:

- Do not feed wildlife.
- Do not pick flowers.
- Do not remove any natural features – including rocks, wood, and antlers.
- Pets must be on a leash and are not permitted on trails.
- Hunting and discharge of firearms is not allowed.
- All food must be stored to protect wildlife.

Firearms and Bear Deterrent Spray

Firearms are now legal in Glacier National Park. This means that you can carry legal firearms, except in federal facilities. However, the use of firearms is prohibited in national parks. Hunting and target practice are also still prohibited in Glacier.

To protect yourself from wildlife, including bear attacks, you should carry bear spray and know how to use it. Bear spray has been proven to be the best method of fending off animals while preventing injury. As bear spray tends to be pricey and you cannot take it home on an airplane with you, there are places in and around Glacier National Park where you can rent bear spray for a small daily fee. It is also available to purchase in most camp stores, for about $50.00.

You can read more about Montana firearms regulations at: **doj.mt.gov/enforcement/concealed-weapons/**.

Fishing

The park stream fishing season is from the third Saturday in May until November 30. Lake fishing is open all year, but there are exceptions in certain areas. There are many places that are closed to fishing all of the time, such as Upper Kintla Lake and Cracker Lake. You do not need a fishing permit to fish in Glacier. However, in some places you will need a Montana state fishing license, such as when fishing from park lands or bridges along the Middle Fork of the Flathead River.

If you plan on fishing in Glacier National Park, be sure to obtain a copy of Glacier National Park's current Fishing Regulations before fishing. There are specific rules as far as the type of fish, the area in Glacier Park, fish consumption, among many other rules that you need to know. You may also need a copy of the Montana Fishing Regulations and in some areas, the Blackfeet Tribal Regulations. If you have any questions, ask a ranger or the nearest Visitor Center.

Fly fishing on the Flathead River

Many Glacier

Chapter Twelve: Equipment and What to Bring

Glacier National Park is WILD. Yes, there are lots of other people, and this is a tourist destination. But there are wild animals, unpredictable weather, cliffs, rushing water, and all things – beautiful and treacherous alike - that come along with nature. Being prepared is critical to having a safe and fun trip.

Too often in Montana and Glacier, the morning starts out sunny with a blue sky and by afternoon it is hailing or snowing. We try to plan ahead and be prepared for inclement weather, or the chance of being stuck overnight, by carrying additional food and gear. Although I sometimes complain while hiking about how heavy our packs are, we live by the motto – "It is better to have it and not need it than to need it and not have it." Of course, carrying children along adds quite a bit of weight between them and the stuff you need to carry for them. Having a packing list before you go will help ensure that you don't leave anything you need behind.

Many items listed below are more critical if you are hiking, or plan on being away from your car. But it never hurts to carry the items with you in your car, just in case.

These items are not necessarily in order of how essential they are for you. Every item here serves a purpose, so take a look at the entire list before packing! If weight or space is an issue, forego some of the less important items and prioritize the essentials.

Bear Spray

This is a book about traveling Glacier with your family. Nothing is more important than keeping your family safe, and this is bear country. Bear spray is the most critical item you must carry while hiking in Glacier. I carry it every time. Although bear attacks are rare, bears are all over the Park, and you might see a bear, or even a mountain lion, at any time.

I recommend every adult in your party carry a can of bear spray when hiking. If possible, hike in groups of at least two, preferably three adults, and walk 30 feet apart when in tight places with obstructed views. We carry a brand called Counter Assault, but the Park stores seem to carry a different brand. I have never had to deploy my spray in the wild, and hope I never have to.

Bear deterrent spray is ready to go

You can purchase bear spray in most general stores in and around the park. You can rent bear spray in Apgar for a minimal daily charge. This is ideal for people who are only planning on doing one or two day hikes and therefore only need spray for a few days. Bear Spray by the bottle is about $50.00; you will only want to buy if you plan on doing a lot of hiking during your trip.

Note that while firearms are now permitted inside Glacier, it is still illegal to discharge a firearm in the Park. Thus, you are not permitted to shoot at a bear, even if you are in danger. Bear spray has also been proven to be the most effective defense in a bear attack.

Water

Water is a no-brainer, yet easily overlooked. We always carry a lot of water in our vehicle, just in case something happens, or if there is some casualty of person or property resulting from young children in the back seat. There are only a few places to purchase or get water inside the Park, (including some campgrounds), so you will want to have extra with you at all times. Bottles of water or a hydropack are a necessity when you are hiking. Montana summers can get hot, up to 90 degrees or more, and you will want to be prepared. Many trails in Glacier are on open, exposed mountainsides, and it is easy to get overheated while hiking. Water is critical in helping to prevent this. Do NOT drink the water in lakes, streams, etc., as the water is not safe to drink, despite the fact that it looks clean and pristine!

Filtering water is recommended

Photo courtesy of Blake Passmore

Extra clothing

We always carry extra clothing, both in the vehicle and when hiking. Layers are the best way to go in Montana, even in the summer. You never know when you might encounter snow, rain, wind, or heat. So be prepared with a warm coat, a raincoat, and dress in layers. When we hike in the summer, we carry about two extra layers per person in case of inclement weather. The extra clothing also comes in handy during breaks to make a cozy picnic spot.

Hiking Shoes / Boots

A good pair of hiking shoes or hiking boots is necessary for hiking in Glacier. Be sure you have worn them before your trip so that they are broken in, and you are not wearing them brand new, or you are sure to have sore feet and blisters! I do a lot of hiking in Glacier, and I do not wear hiking boots. I wear a good pair of trail running shoes, and they serve my purpose. For most people visiting Glacier, a good pair of running shoes with aggressive soles will work just fine for your hiking. Hiking boots to me are heavy and make my feet so hot in the middle of the summer that I choose to stick with my trusty sneakers.

The Glacier Park trail crew does an amazing job keeping the trails in great shape, and as all the hikes listed in this book are fairly mild, I never use special hiking boots for any of them.

Basic First Aid Kit

We always carry a very basic first aid kit in our backpack while hiking, just in case, and it doesn't take up much space in the backpack. It is also a good item to have in your vehicle.

Leatherman Multi-tool

A Leatherman Multi-tool is an item that has multiple tools on it including a knife, pliers, can opener, bottle opener, file, saw, screwdrivers, and scissors. This tool has so many purposes, especially if you will be going into the backcountry at all. This small tool takes up so little space and could be just the thing for any number of needs when out in the wild with your family.

Sunscreen

Montana summers are hot, and a lot of hikes in Glacier are on exposed hillsides with no trees or shade. Don't overlook this basic item, especially for little ones.

Sunglasses / Hat

You will be visiting higher elevations in Glacier, and you won't always have access to shade. The occasional wind can be tough on eyes, and sunlight can reflect particularly well off of glaciers and snow, shale rock, and alpine lakes. Be prepared by carrying these items with you.

Small Soft Cooler for Hiking

We always carry a small soft cooler to carry our lunch and snacks in. A soft-sided cooler – as opposed to a hard cooler – fits more easily into a backpack. We have recently started carrying so many items with two small children that we now attach our cooler to the outside of our Deuter backpack to provide us with more space for other items inside our packs. We also carry our youngest child in an Osprey Poco Plus kids carrier. See Chapter Thirteen for a discussion about the child carriers we use for backpacking with small children. Whether you pack your cooler in the backpack or carry it separate, we have found this cooler to be a necessity. The one we carry is just 7" x 8" x 10" and only cost about $10, but it is more than enough to carry our lunches, our children's lunch and snacks, including yogurt, drinks, and string cheese. You will also want a small ice pack to throw in to keep everything cold for several hours.

Small plastic garbage bags

We refer to this necessity as our "little blue bags." Having them be the color blue, of course, serves no purpose. That just happens to be the color that I buy. I buy these in the baby aisle; they sell on-the-go garbage bags for diapers, and are meant to attach to a diaper bag. Yes, these small bags are great to put your diapers in while hiking to get them back without making a mess in your pack. But they are also great for food garbage, toilet paper, wet swimming suits, and any multitude of items left in the wake of a family hike. They are sold rolled up in a very small bundle so they don't take up space, or you can just rip off a couple to carry in your pack. You won't regret bringing this item, even if you just keep them in your vehicle!

Kelty Tarp

We love carrying a waterproof thin tarp made by Kelty with us everywhere we go. These tarps can be used to make a quick shelter from rain (or sun), but we mostly use ours to sit on in the woods to keep everyone dry, and keep gear somewhat organized. These are great to have in your vehicle if you want to stop for a picnic, but we always carry ours in our backpack. The one we use is compact, thin, lightweight, and can really make your hike more enjoyable when you stop for breaks with kids and the ground is damp.

Big Cooler for your Vehicle

Driving anywhere in Glacier can take several hours, depending on how many times you stop to hike, picnic, take photos, and stop for a stretch. I recommend carrying a larger cooler in your vehicle to carry extra drinks, food, and anything else you want to keep cool. You can only purchase food and water at a limited number of areas in the Park, so you will want to carry these things with you at all times. Food is not available for purchase at Logan Pass, so you will want to stock up at Rising Sun and Lake McDonald Lodge on either side of Logan Pass, if you have not already done so at West Glacier or St. Mary.

Digital Camera and Accessories

A digital camera is clearly a mandatory item to have on your trip to Glacier. The scenery is some of the best in the world. I see a lot of people taking their photos on their IPads and IPhones. While I am a big fan of taking photos on IPhones for convenience (you need to be able to immediately upload them to social media, right?!), IPads to me are large and cumbersome. Be sure to invest in a small, good digital camera to bring on your trip. Of course, large and expensive cameras may better capture the majesty of this Crown of the Continent, but may prove too cumbersome and heavy given all the other gear you may need, on even a short hike.

Capture your memories on camera

Also be sure to bring a couple of SD Memory Cards, because you will want plenty of space for photos. A mini-tripod that can fit in your pack is also great for taking steady photos, and for taking photos when no one else is around so that you are able to get the entire family in the shot using self-timers. Make sure your camera is charged! Perhaps a hazard of having Glacier out our back door and occasionally taking for granted the fact we visit dozens of times per year, we have raced out the door with an empty card slot, no juice in the battery, or no battery at all. Do not make this mistake if visiting Glacier is a rare privilege.

Water Shoes / Keens for adults and kids

Water shoes are nice to have while traveling in Glacier, and Keens are the brand that I like for children. Any water shoe is handy for the lakes and streams in the Park. I have loved Keens for my children because they have good traction on the bottom but are not as hot as sneakers in the summer, and then they can be in the water as well without changing shoes. I prefer myself to wear water shoes like Tevas, which don't make my feet as hot and don't keep them wet for long periods after I get the shoe wet like Keens do. If you are planning on doing any fishing, Keens are a great shoe because they offer toe protection from the rocks as you walk around in the rivers.

Cell Phone Charger

While there is not a lot of cell service in the park, it seems that everyone takes their photos with their iPhones these days. If your iPhone battery drains while you are hiking in Glacier, a portable external battery charger is convenient to have. These only require a battery, are inexpensive, and it allows you to plug in your phone to charge it on the go. Their small size makes them easy to pack.

Space Blanket

A space blanket is extremely compact and is an item that can be used if you get in a bind while hiking or traveling around Glacier. We always carry two in our backpacks while hiking.

Bug Spray

We also carry a small container of mosquito spray with us in our backpack, although we have rarely had to use it. Sometimes you might experience a lot of mosquitoes near lakes or streams. If you have a small bit of extra space, you should bring bug spray, mostly because this may save you from having a miserable time in case you do encounter bugs.

SteriPen

We carry a SteriPen while hiking, just in case of emergency or other delay and we run out of water. A SteriPen is a handheld water purification system that you can easily pack in a backpack. You should not drink the water in Glacier, due to the possibility of catching Giardia, or other microorganisms. A SteriPen (or a pot to boil water, if you have one) will make the water safe to drink if you run out of water and need more in the backcountry when you don't have access to treated or clean water.

Extra Fuel

You cannot get fuel anywhere inside of the Park. You have to get it before you enter the Park. Be sure to fill up your gas tank before entering, as you will be doing a lot of driving in Glacier.

Warm Hat

In addition to wearing layers and being prepared, a warm hat is smart to have. Just in case you are

Mountain goats on the Avalanche Lake Trail

stuck outside overnight, you won't regret having items to keep you warmer at higher elevations. Hats are also great for camping on chilly nights, even in the summer. The random rain or hailstorm in the middle of summer is also great opportunities for winter hats.

Binoculars

A pair of binoculars is something I often forget to bring hiking, although we always carry a set in our truck. Binoculars really come in handy when you want to look for mountain goats at Logan Pass, or grizzly bears at Many Glacier. Carrying a very small pair in your backpack while hiking might help you get more views of wildlife. This, like a large digital camera, is one of those items you will have to decide its value given the additional space and weight in what may be an otherwise crammed gear list.

Flashlight

A small flashlight is a fairly light item that will come in handy if you are stranded in your vehicle or have to spend the night in the woods. If you have an emergency and had to stay in the woods for a night, you do not want to be out there without light. We carry one in our vehicle, and a very small one in our packs.

Radios or Walkie Talkies

Walkie Talkies are not something I carry on a regular basis, but these could be handy in the Park because there is very little cell service coverage. This would allow you to keep in touch with your party or get in touch if you split up. There are obviously mountains everywhere to block signals, so be cautious of the range you might expect.

Backpacks

Backpacks are a necessity for hiking, in order to carry all this gear. (For information on hiking carriers for children, see the next section on equipment to carry with young children.) There are many brands available. Choose one that is lightweight, has several pockets for various gear, and that is large enough for all the gear you need to carry for yourself and your family.

Parachute Cord

Parachute cord has become popular, and is so light to carry if you go on longer hikes in case you need emergency shelter, tie downs, 1st aid, etc.

Small Umbrella

We sometimes carry a small umbrella to stuff in our backpack in case we get caught in the rain. We often choose to carry either this or the Kelty Tarp for quick rain shelter for the kids.

The above list is for general family hikes and outings of about 10 miles or less. Overnight trips, longer backcountry trips, or aggressive cliffs would obviously require additional gear that I have not listed here.

McDonald Creek in the fall

McDonald Creek

Chapter Thirteen: Equipment for Young Children

Traveling and camping with young children can be a handful, but we have embraced it and just taken them along for the ride. Glacier National Park can be enjoyed with small children, but it is beneficial to bring appropriate equipment for really little ones.

Kid Carrier Backpack

A backpack that carries a kid and gives you extra room to carry items for your hike is critical for allowing you to hike with children. Our favorite is the Deuter Kid Comfort III child carrier, but most brands will work just fine. Some of my favorite features are: a small rearview hand mirror to check on children, shoulder harness adjusts to fit either parents torso length, foldout stand to set the pack on the ground, large zippered pockets, raincover/sunroof, 5-point adjustable harness for child, high back that provides protection in case of falls, chin pad that removes to wash, and side mesh pockets to hold sippy cups. We also have and like the Osprey Poco Plus.

Ergobaby Baby Carrier (with infant insert)

The Ergobaby is a fantastic baby carrier that can carry children up to 45 pounds. If you buy the infant insert, you can start carrying babies in this at 7 pounds. The carrier allows you to carry your baby on your front or back or your hip. The Ergobaby 360 now allows you to carry your child outward facing or inward facing. The shoulder pads on this carrier provide good support for hiking with kids, making it more comfortable than products like the Baby Bjorn for hiking. Your baby will most likely happily sleep in this carrier.

Diapers and wipes

Packing diapers and wipes seems like a no-brainer if you are traveling with small children. However, finding these products in and around Glacier National Park will prove nearly impossible in most locations. Bring what you need, or be sure to shop in larger grocery stores in nearby Kalispell, Columbia Falls, or Whitefish. We also carry ultra-compact wipes for backup. These are the size of a dime, and expand when you add water.

Liquid formula (even if nursing, as backup)

Liquid formula is nice to have as backup, and doesn't require you to carry extra water to mix formula. Just like diapers, formula is difficult to find in and around Glacier. Be sure to stock up at larger grocery stores in nearby towns.

Keens or wet/dry shoes

Children will need shoes that can get wet. While traveling and hiking around Glacier National Park, we love Keens as a water shoe for small children. It lets some air flow into their feet, although their feet do tend to be sweaty in these shoes. It provides good traction for walking around and they can wade into any water and you don't have to worry about how wet their feet get! Since you will be carrying small children on most hikes, they don't need hiking shoes like the adults do.

Sun Hats for Kids

Montana summers can be hot, and a sun hat will help provide protection against the sun, especially in exposed areas like Logan Pass.

Snacks On the Go

Easy, on-the-go, snacks are critical for small children. Anyone with a

That's a lot of gear

baby or toddler knows that if they are hungry, they are not happy. So be sure to bring food that is easy to pack, preferably does not spoil, and is something they enjoy. We prefer to carry nuts, but things like Goldfish may be a good option. (My father-in-law is a dentist, and he would prefer kids don't eat Goldfish unless you can brush their teeth directly afterward!) We break out some chocolate when our kids just do not want to be in the backpack any more on the longer hikes.

Blanket / stuffed animal

My children's blankets, stuffed animals, and baby dolls have been all over Glacier National Park and Yellowstone National Park. These items are of utmost importance. Once while hiking in Yellowstone National Park, we had just returned to our vehicle after a hike, and we realized we had dropped our child's favorite stuffed beaver. My husband ran the entire hike again just to find Benny the Beaver all the way back at the lake.

Mesh wrap

Mesh wraps are a great option for small babies because they are comfortable and cooler in the middle of the summer. The lightweight material allows baby to stay cool, and you can wear this in the water if you are around lakes in Glacier. I recommend Beachfront baby wraps.

Boppy Lounger for car/picnic use

The Newborn Lounger made by Boppy is one of my favorite products. This is such a nice place to set babies while you are camping or having a picnic. This is convenient for small babies who cannot roll yet. One of the only downsides to it is that the cover is not removable for washing. Of course, never leave your child unattended with any baby product like this.

Baby Bjorn

The Baby Bjorn carrier is a good carrier for very small children. Smaller babies will be cozy, and children who can support their own head can also face outward. The one downside with this carrier is that there is not a lot of shoulder support, so it will wear on you if you carry them in this on longer hikes.

Swaddle Blankets

I can't tell you how much use we have gotten out of our Aden and Anais swaddle blankets. These blankets are nice and thin, making them ideal for the summer heat. We use them as blankets, as shade from the sun, to sit on, etc. These make great summer baby blankets.

Crossing the Paradise Creek Bridge

A Red Bus crosses the bridge over Haystack Creek

Photo courtesy of Blake Passmore

Chapter 14: Sample Itineraries

ONE DAY

From Highway 2 in West Glacier, enter the Park and follow the signs to Apgar Village, and take in the iconic view from the south shore of Lake McDonald. Get back on Going-to-the-Sun Road and follow it along Lake McDonald, McDonald Creek, and then up, up, up, toward Logan Pass. Take advantage of the multiple pullouts along the way. At Logan Pass, be on the lookout for mountain goats and bighorn sheep. Stretch your legs in the visitor center and stroll the trails behind it. If you want more than a quick leg stretch, take the easy 1.5 mile walk up to Hidden Lake overlook. Back in your car, follow the signs down the east side of the pass toward Saint Mary.

Once at Saint Mary, turn north and follow the signs toward Babb and Many Glacier. While you may be satisfied with your awesome Going-to-the-Sun Road experience and tempted to be on your way, don't skip this 30-45 minute (one way) detour. It will take you to the "heart" of Glacier, offering not only spectacular views, but also your best chance to see bears from the road. In the course of one mid-September day, we saw black bears, grizzly bears, bighorn sheep, mountain goats, moose, and elk, all from the road! Of course spotting wildlife is never guaranteed, but other than goats and sheep at Logan Pass, this is probably your best chance in Glacier.

Back at Saint Mary, if you still have some time and want to explore just a bit more from your car, take Hwy 49 toward East Glacier and drive up the Two Medicine Valley.

This will make for a long, full day in the car.

Approximate drive times, without any stopping, are: West Glacier to Logan Pass – about 90 minutes; Logan Pass to Saint Mary – about 30 minutes; Saint Mary to Many Glacier – about 45 minutes; Two Medicine from East Glacier – about 30 minutes; East Glacier to West Glacier via Highway 2 – about 60 minutes.

Add a Hike to Your Drive

Option 1 - Hidden Lake Overlook – expansive views; easy 1.5 mile hike; leaves from Logan Pass; good chance to see mountain goats.

Option 2 – Trail of the Cedars/Avalanche Lake – Massive Cedar trees and creek/waterfalls if you just do the easy .9 mile Trail of the Cedars loop, which is stroller and wheelchair friendly. Avalanche Lake adds another approximately 45 minutes, one way.

*If you visit in July or August, parking at Avalanche and Logan Pass is very congested between 9:00 a.m. and 5:00 p.m., so plan accordingly.

TWO DAYS

<u>Day 1</u> – Lake McDonald Valley and Going-to-the-Sun Road. Hike Trail of the Cedars/Avalanche Lake; Hike Hidden Lake Overlook. If you want additional hiking, do St. Mary Falls/Virginia Falls. If one or two hikes is enough, take a boat tour of Lake McDonald or Saint Mary.

<u>Overnight</u> – If camping, stay at Apgar, Fish Creek, Rising Sun or Saint Mary. Keep in mind that Saint Mary and Fish Creek accept reservations, and many of the campgrounds fill before noon, with Many Glacier and Two Medicine often filling early in the morning. If you plan to stay in a hotel, try to book ahead and treat yourself to a night in the Many Glacier Hotel – its pricy, but worth it for a night.

<u>Day 2</u> – Many Glacier. Take the early boat tour across Swiftcurrent Lake and Lake Josephine, and take the easy .9 mile hike to Grinnell Lake. Upon return, grab lunch at the Many Glacier Hotel, and watch for bears on the hillside above the hotel – even in the middle of the day. Then, drive the short distance to the end of the road to the Swiftcurrent Motor Inn and hike up to Red Rock Falls. This is an easy 45-minute, 4-mile hike, and offers gorgeous waterfalls, a great snack spot at Red Rock Lake, and your best chance of seeing moose if you take the 2-minute detour down to Fishercap Lake.

THREE DAYS

<u>Day 1, 1st Overnight, and Day 2</u> – See the 2-day itinerary above.

<u>2nd Overnight</u> – Camp at Two Medicine, or stay in the Glacier Park Lodge in East Glacier Park. If you don't want to change hotels/campsites, base out of either Many Glacier, Apgar, or Saint Mary. Two Medicine/East Glacier is a bit out of the way – so is Many Glacier, but there is more to do and more accommodations there.

<u>Day 3 – Two Medicine</u> – Take a boat tour across Two Medicine Lake, and take the two easy hikes to Twin Falls and Upper Two Medicine Lake. After the boat tour, get a snack at the store – there is no formal restaurant here – and hike up to Aster Falls and Aster Park Overlook, taking the short detour down to Paradise Point on your way back. Or, if you've had enough hiking and want to splash around, the east end of Pray Lake (by the campground) and the creek between Two Medicine Lake and Pray Lake (also along the Two Medicine Campground) can provide hours of fun, with amazing views to boot.

<u>Option 2</u> – Spend an extra day at Many Glacier and hike to Iceberg Lake. Then, drive up Two Medicine Valley to explore the lake and campground, and take the short stroll over to Running Eagle Falls, which is stroller and wheelchair friendly.

> We often debate whether Two Medicine or Many Glacier is our favorite part of the Park. Most visitors – based simply on number of people we see – seem to prefer Many Glacier. So if you want the climax of the trip to come last, do Many Glacier last. But don't skip Two Medicine – though the campground gets crowded, this area just feels quieter.

A Red Bus at parked at the Bird Woman Falls viewpoint

FOUR DAYS

Day 1 – Lake McDonald Valley and Going-to-the-Sun Road.

1st Overnight – Camp at Apgar, or stay at Lake McDonald Lodge or Village Inn. Be at Lake McDonald for sunset.

Day 2 – Two Medicine. See activities under 3-day itinerary above. For all day hiking, skip the return trip on the boat, and follow the South Shore trail to catch Rockwell Falls, Aster Park, and Aster Falls.

2nd Overnight – Camp at Two Medicine, or stay in the Glacier Park Lodge in East Glacier Park. If camping get to the campground no later than mid-morning during the busy season.

Day 3 – Many Glacier. Hike to Iceberg Lake in the morning; Upon return in late-afternoon, Stroll around the Swiftcurrent Nature Trail, rent a kayak, or get a pony ride if you have small children.

3rd Overnight – Camp at Many Glacier, or stay at the Many Glacier Hotel or Swiftcurrent Motor Inn. If camping, get to the campground no later than 8:00 a.m. during the busy season. Many Glacier Campground is a zoo in the mornings during July, August, and even into September, and finding a spot can be stressful. If your plans or other limitations prevent you from arriving early, book a hotel or camp at Saint Mary.

Day 4 – Many Glacier - Morning boat tour and short hike to Grinnell Lake; Hike up to Redrock Falls.

FIVE DAYS

Day 1 – Lake McDonald Valley and Going-to-the-Sun Road.

1st Overnight – Camp at Apgar, or stay at Lake McDonald Lodge or Village Inn. Be at Lake McDonald for sunset.

Day 2 – Two Medicine

2nd Overnight – Camp at Two Medicine, or stay in the Glacier Park Lodge in East Glacier Park. If camping get to the campground no later than mid-morning during the busy season.

Day 3 – Many Glacier – Hike to Iceberg Lake in the morning; Rent a kayak or rowboat and play on Swiftcurrent Lake in the afternoon and evening.

3rd Overnight – Camp at Many Glacier, or stay at the Many Glacier Hotel or Swiftcurrent Motor Inn. If camping, get to the campground no later than 8:00 a.m. during the busy season. Many Glacier Campground is a zoo in the mornings during July, August, and even into September, and finding a spot can be stressful. If your plans or other limitations prevent you from arriving early, book a hotel or camp at Saint Mary.

Day 4 – Many Glacier – Hike or Horseback ride to Cracker Lake; Stroll up to Fishercap Lake in the evening to look for moose.

4th Overnight – Camp at Many Glacier, or stay at the Many Glacier Hotel or Swiftcurrent Motor Inn.

Day 5 – Many Glacier – Morning boat tour and short hike to Grinnell Lake; Hike up to Redrock Falls

SIX DAYS

Day 1 – Lake McDonald Valley and Going-to-the-Sun Road.

1st Overnight – Camp at Apgar or Fish Creek, or stay at Lake McDonald Lodge or Village Inn. Be at Lake McDonald for sunset.

Day 2 –Explore the North Fork – Get up early and drive up to Bowman Lake, and get a treat at the Polebridge Mercantile along the way. If you want some additional gravel road exploration, drive up to Kintla Lake.

2nd Overnight – Camp at Two Medicine, or stay in the Glacier Park Lodge in East Glacier Park. Remember, if you plan to camp at Two Medicine you must get to the campground no later than mid-morning during the busy season. If you plan to spend more than half the day in the North Fork and are camping, you should either camp at Bowman Lake, Kintla Lake, or stay camped at Apgar or Fish Creek.

Day 3 – Two Medicine -

3rd Overnight - Camp at Two Medicine, or stay in the Glacier Park Lodge in East Glacier Park. If camping get to the campground no later than mid-morning during the busy season.

Day 4 – Many Glacier – Hike to Iceberg Lake in the morning; Rent a kayak or rowboat and play on Swiftcurrent Lake in the afternoon and evening.

4th Overnight – Camp at Many Glacier, or stay at the Many Glacier Hotel or Swiftcurrent Motor Inn. If camping, get to the campground no later than 8:00 a.m. during the busy season. Many Glacier Campground is a zoo in the mornings during July, August, and even into September, and finding a spot can be stressful. If your plans or other limitations prevent you from arriving early, book a hotel or camp at Saint Mary.

Day 5 – Many Glacier – Hike or Horseback ride to Cracker Lake; Stroll up to Fishercap Lake in the evening to look for moose.

5th Overnight – Camp at Many Glacier, or stay at the Many Glacier Hotel or Swiftcurrent Motor Inn.

Day 6 – Many Glacier – Morning boat tour and short hike to Grinnell Lake; Hike up to Redrock Falls

SEVEN DAYS OR MORE

Use the 6-day itinerary above. Add in a half-day or full-day Red Bus Tour, add another horseback ride, or free pony rides for younger children, or explore some of the sights and attractions in the Flathead Valley. Spend the extra night in the Two Medicine area.

Recommended Top Ten Hikes For Families:

The following is a list of the top ten hikes for families. Some are easier and some are more difficult, but they are all worth hiking and many of them can be done by younger children on their own. None of the hikes on this list will disappoint, as they each provide unique features and views.

1. Red Rock Lake/Falls   page 58

2. Grinnell Lake   page 52

3. Hidden Lake   page 21

4. Iceberg Lake   page 55

5. Avalanche Lake   page 26

6. Grinnell Glacier   page 53

7. Swiftcurrent Nature Trail/Lake Josephine   page 52

8. St. Mary Falls/Virginia Falls   page 69

9. Twin Falls/Upper Two Medicine Lake   page 42

10. Aster Falls/Rockwell Falls   page 41

Avalanche Lake